Brand Identity in Sport

Brand Identity in Sport

Jason W. Lee

Susan Westcott Alessandri

Carolina Academic Press

Durham, North Carolina

Library of Congress Cataloging-in-Publication Data

Names: Lee, Jason W., author. | Alessandri, Susan Westcott, author.
Title: Brand identity in sport / Jason W. Lee and Susan Westcott Alessandri.
Description: Durham, North Carolina : Carolina Academic Press, LLC, [2018] |
Includes bibliographical references and index.
Identifiers: LCCN 2017052808 | ISBN 9781531000097 (alk. paper)
Subjects: LCSH: Sports--Marketing--Research. | Sports--Social aspects. |
Sports--Economic aspects.
Classification: LCC GV716 .L42 2018 | DDC 338.4/779--dc23
LC record available at https://lccn.loc.gov/2017052808

eISBN 978-1-53100-010-3

p 3, "Name tag" icon by Creative Stall, from thenounproject.com.
p 17, "Shield" icon by Martin Smith, from thenounproject.com.
p 27, "Paint Swatches" icon by ProSymbols, from thenounproject.com.
p 39, "Construction" icon by Creative Stall, from thenounproject.com.
p 49, "Football Uniform" icon by Lilit Kalachyan, from thenounproject.com.
p 59, "Running" icon by James Fenton, from thenounproject.com.
p 77, "Protest" icon by Juan Pablo Bravo, from thenounproject.com.
p 87, "Intellectual Property" icon by USPTO, from thenounproject.com.
p 99, "Feedback" icon by dilakuscan, from thenounproject.com.
p 101, "Checklist" icon by Davo Sime, from thenounproject.com.
p 107, "Megaphone" icon by Luis Prado, from thenounproject.com.

Carolina Academic Press, LLC
700 Kent Street
Durham, North Carolina 27701
Telephone (919) 489-7486
Fax (919) 493-5668
www.cap-press.com

Printed in the United States of America

I want to thank everyone who has helped me establish my brand identity. In particular, I want to thank my mom, my sons Matthew and Andrew, and Karen for helping me be all that I can be.
—JWL

To Cambria Alona Alessandri, my little lover of books.
I'm sure your critique will be spot-on.
—SWA

Contents

Introduction

What Is Brand Identity in Sport?

An Introduction to Brand Identity and Its Role in Sport

On Nov. 9, 2012, National Collegiate Athletic Association (NCAA) Division I college basketball teams met in Germany to participate in the first-ever Armed Forces Classic, held on location at Ramstein Air Base. This followed the popular 2011 "Carrier Classic," a basketball matchup between Michigan State University and the University of North Carolina at Chapel Hill held aboard the aircraft carrier USS *Carl Vinson* in San Diego. While these events show an interesting crossover between college athletes and their military counterparts, brand identity practitioners and scholars likely noticed how these events illustrated several important brand identity concepts.

Brand identity encompasses how an organization presents itself, which might manifest itself in many ways. Specifically, an organization's brand identity is defined as its strategically planned and purposeful presentation of itself in order to gain a positive image, and ultimately a positive reputation (Alessandri, 2009). Operationally, an organization's brand identity is its name, logo, tagline, color palette, and several other tactical elements that serve to identify and promote the organization. These include the organization's architecture, interior design, mascots, and even "non-brand" elements such as scents and sounds. Broadly speaking, anything that is used to identify the organization in a sensory way—that is, seeing, hearing, smelling, touching and perhaps even tasting—is part of that organization's *brand identity*.

In the case of these basketball match-ups, the teams and the universities they represented were projecting their brand identities through their uniforms. The Nike-sponsored schools knew they were playing a different kind of game, and Nike knew they needed a different kind of uniform. Taking a page from a military strategy manual, the teams were outfitted in "camo" patterned uniforms in the traditional colors of their respective universities. While this might seem gimmicky on its face, the decision to slightly redesign the uniform illustrates very clearly that the teams—and most certainly Nike—understand that brand identity, and hence presentation, matters. One of the most immediate ways to make an organization known to the public is to associate it with one or more brand and/or sensory elements. It becomes a type of sensory shorthand to aid recognition and association, which can result in exponential benefits for the organization.

An organization's brand identity elements serve various purposes. In sport, they provide a means for identity, recognition, and even "community"—as they can serve to bind individuals together and differentiate groups from others. In sport, particularly collegiate athletics, the use of such brand identity elements are used to achieve solidarity and community for a wide assortment of stakeholders, such as student-athletes, students, faculty, staff members, administrators, boosters, corporate partners, the surrounding community, and various other stakeholder groups. Non-academic sport entities also have various stakeholders including fans, local citizens, ownership, management, media, business partners, and others.

Consider the following representative examples: institutions adopt nicknames for their athletic teams (e.g., University of Arkansas Razorbacks); fans display the team colors (e.g., the garnet and gold of Florida State University); proudly wave flags (e.g., flying the burnt orange flag for the Texas Longhorn symbol of the University of Texas); dress in consumer apparel (e.g., mountaineer attire at West Virginia University football games); and yell out "battle cries," slogans, etc. (e.g., Oklahoma University fans yelling "Boomer Sooner").

Though the preceding examples are representative of well-known intercollegiate experiences, similar traditions, actions, and activities occur in other segments of sport, including professional sport and interscholastic sport. In professional sport, there are notable examples, including the Green Bay Packer "Cheeseheads," the outlandish antics of the Portland Timbers Army fan group, the tomahawk chop of the Atlanta Braves, the presence of the Dallas Cowboys Cheerleaders, the outlandish attire of certain Oakland Raider fans that comprise its notorious "Black Hole," the throwing of the octopi at Detroit Red Wings games, and the list goes on. Each of these experiences is rooted in—and is a central part of—the team's brand identity. Fans who identify strongly with their teams are often driven to personify the brand, either by action or by apparel. The beauty of a strong brand identity is that it helps to fortify a fan's loyalty while simultaneously strengthening the brand identity for the organization.

Benefits and Foundations of Brand Identity

The benefits of a positive and well-received brand identity are both varied and many. From fans that wear team apparel, furthering perpetuating public awareness of the brand, to vendors who wish to sell apparel, thereby increasing the licensing portfolio of the brand itself, a strategically planned, promoted, and protected brand identity is the core, the centerpiece of an organization's brand and marketing programs.

A truly superior brand identity is strategically built on the history, beliefs, or traditions of the organization. The brand identity's meaning should be reasonably apparent to those familiar with the organization, and the best brand identities will remain true to the organization even through changes in the short- and long-term because they were built with some sort of guiding statements, such as the organization's mission statement or a long-term vision statement.

Examinations of various core brand identity elements are addressed in upcoming chapters. This includes an examination of the primary elements, such as names, logos, color palettes, and more. Beyond these, other key brand identity elements are addressed throughout this book. This includes the concept of taglines. Taglines are addressed in the subsequent section.

Consider Taglines

Sport organizations use taglines as memorable communication shorthand, and in the sports context they are typically referred to as slogans, battle cries, or mottos. Regardless of what they are called, taglines are powerful communication tools because they have the potential to grow into strong and positive identifiers for sport organizations of all sizes and types. Taglines serve as a means for reflecting a brand's promise by summarizing the character of whatever is advertised. Specifically, "taglines are composed of concise statements that are aimed at accomplishing goals such as gaining attention, sending a message, and prompting consumers to action" (Lee, 2011d, p. 1519). Famous sport taglines have been used to identify or advertise brands through associations that are closely tied to the product represented, such as:

- Nike: "Just Do It"
- EA Sports: "It's in the Game"
- ESPN: "The Worldwide Leader in Sports"

Colleges and universities also employ taglines in marketing communications. The following are some sample university taglines:

- Baylor University: "Above. Beyond."
- Berry College: "A Foundation for Life"
- Troy University: "A Future of Opportunities"
- University of North Florida: "No One Like You. No Place Like This."

Other taglines, of sorts, have been uttered, or "invented," by individuals and entered common vernacular. Some of these have gone on to receive trademark protection:

- Pat Riley, former coach of the NBA's Los Angeles Lakers: "Threepeat"
- Michael Buffer, professional ring announcer: "Let's Get Ready to Rumble"
- NCAA: "March Madness"
- New England Patriots: "Blitz for Six" (Rovell, 2017)

Such messages can serve as strong identifiers and convey desired messages to stakeholders. These can also be projected through the use of brand identity touchpoints, such as apparel, business communications, social media, and merchandise.

Aside from the previously mentioned taglines, there are a plethora of brand identity elements that impact the sport industry. While detailed discussion and examples are provided for various core brand identity elements in the forthcoming chapter, Table 1 provides an introductory listing of core brand identity elements. Table 2 provides a listing of touchpoints. Brand touchpoints are those tactics that organizations employ to project elements of their brand identities. Examples might include marketing communications, business communications, apparel, etc. For additional examples, refer to Appendices 1 and 2 in the back of the book.

Integration Is Key

Although touchpoints may be traditional or exotic, what they always need to be is consistent and integrated with one another. Most people need to hear, see, or experience something more than once to truly understand it. For example, when an ad appears on television, the viewer might not see the entire message the first time, or they may hear the spot while busy doing something else, so they don't actually see the content. It could take a few exposures before they can actively process the message. Marketers generally understand that integration of messages is important, and from a brand identity perspective, the idea that stakeholders will see consistent messages across media is vital to maintaining the integrity of the identity. The concept of Integrated Marketing Communications (IMC) satisfies this need (Schultz, Tannenbaum, and Lauterborn, 1993).

The promise of an IMC approach is that integrated communication, based on stakeholder needs, will separate one organization from another by associating the organization with value in the minds of the public.

Table 1: Core Brand Identity Elements

Names	Organization College or University Conference Team Stadium or venue Nickname(s) (official and unofficial)
Logos	Primary marks Secondary marks Wordmarks (typography) Crests Seals/emblems
Color Palettes	Primary colors Secondary colors Tertiary colors
Mascots	Physical mascots (people, costumes, animals) Mascot images (cartoons, images, logos)
Buildings, Architecture, and Interior Design	Buildings Architecture Interior décor Sport venues/Sportscape *Settings:* Venues/stadia Headquarters (e.g., athletic department buildings, corporate headquarters) Other academic buildings, statues, art structures, etc.

Table 2: Examples of Brand Touchpoints

Business Communications	Business cards ID Cards Name Tags Letterhead Presentation slides (PPT, Prezi, etc.)
Advertisement	Signage Commercials Ad Spots (online) Brochures Viewbooks
Ephemera/Swag	Promotional items Premiums Giveaways
Uniforms	Work uniforms Athletic uniforms Customary attire Ceremonial garb
Vehicles	Company vehicles Busses Work vehicles Public transit
Web and Social Media	School website Athletic website Social media Apps
Wordage/Phrasing	Positioning statements Taglines Guiding principles Slogans Chants/cheers/Songs/battle cries Mission statement Vision statement

Table 2: Examples of Brand Touchpoints, *continued*

People	Athletes, coaches, administrators, bands, dance squads, cheerleaders, ensnared fans, etc.
Organizational Cultural Forms (Behaviors)*	Symbols (objects, settings, performers) Languages (jargon, gestures, songs, humor, metaphor, proverbs) Narratives (stories, legends, sagas, myths) Practices (rituals, taboos, rites, practices)

* *(Derived from Trice & Beyer, 1993)*

Conclusion

The remainder of this book is divided into chapters that address specific brand identity elements as they pertain to the world of sport. The chapters will provide additional details on core organizational brand identity elements, such as names (Chapter 1); logos and mascots (Chapter 2); colors (Chapter 3); architecture, landscaping, and interior design and decor (Chapter 4); and uniforms and game day rituals (Chapter 5). Chapter 6 provides additional coverage of key brand identity considerations by examining the brand identity-related application of actions and behaviors of organizations and individuals associated with the organizations. Chapter 7 addresses further examinations of how brand identity "touchpoints" project identity, and in turn affect the organization's image and reputation. Chapter 8, the summary chapter, provides a deeper look into the practice and benefits of brand identity licensing as well as the legal and intellectual property rights involved in organizational brand identity.

Part 1

The Elements of Brand Identity

Chapter 1

Names

Organizational names are the primary and key components of any organization's overall brand identity. Names are important marketing assets since they can produce awareness and create a memorable identity (Fetchko, Roy & Clow, 2013). An organization's name is also the element that is referenced most often by fans, the media, and the general public, and it is typically communicated both visually and aurally in communications. Accordingly, names convey messages that can provide added value and influence the organization's brand equity (Hussain & Ferdous, 2015). Names add value because stakeholders form brand associations, or mental links, tied to the given brand (Aaker, 1991; Keller, 1993).

To determine their potential for contribution to brand building, Fetchko, Roy, and Clow (2013) evaluate brand names on three criteria: recognizability, fit, and contrast. Recognizability refers to whether a name provides an apparent association with the given product. Secondly, fit refers to the notion of whether the name matches characteristics of the specific market (e.g., geography, personality). Thirdly, contrast refers to the notion of a name providing differentiation from competitors/referent others.

An appropriate name is one that is well thought out and one that results from strategic thinking about the team or organization. The "right" name for a team can depend on myriad factors, including the type of sport, the history of the team's location, a school's name or benefactor, etc. Such names evoke much more than merely a nominative label, as they symbolically convey the attributes and characteristics of the team or larger organization. Truly unique team names may represent a range of ideas and concepts, including ethnic heritage, regional/state history, religious affiliation, and vocational attributes. Beyond these, there are abounding examples of standby names that reflect attributes such as aggression or ferocity as they relate to animals (e.g., Bears, Bulldogs, or Tigers) or even humans (e.g., Pirates, Cowboys, Vikings). Most team names tend to fall into one of several categories. Although the following list is not exhaustive, the examples provide a broad glimpse into the sport landscape.

Founders & Benefactors. Colleges and universities have generally been in existence longer than any of the people associated with the athletic programs, so naming is not typically an issue, but universities are the best examples of teams that are named after their founders. Teams at Vanderbilt University, Duke University, Butler University, and Baylor University are all examples of eponymous names. Teams and athletes for the Harvard Crimson are representing a university named after the man, John Harvard, who donated the first books to the school's library.

Descriptive. Many professional teams, especially those formed through league expansion or those moving from one geographic location to another, are often able to create new names for themselves. When the NBA's Vancouver Grizzlies were granted the right to relocate to Memphis, Tennessee, in 2001, rumors floated that the team would be named Memphis Express (with team colors of purple and orange) after the city's famous corporate resident, shipping giant FedEx, which also held naming rights to the arena (Associated Press, 2001). While the NBA does not allow teams to be named after corporate sponsors, several teams across sport have chosen names that pay homage to or describe their geographic locale: The Miami Heat (NBA), Carolina Hurricanes (NHL), Pittsburgh Steelers and the San Francisco 49ers (both of the NFL), and the Milwaukee Brewers and Colorado Rockies (both of the MLB), to name some.

Historical. Some professional sport organizations draw upon the historical roots of their hometowns to name their teams. For example, the NFL's New England Patriots celebrate the birthplace of the American Revolution, as does the region's MLS soccer team, the New England Revolution. The San Francisco 49ers name evokes a connection to the region's Gold Rush of 1849, and the Pittsburgh Steelers celebrate the history of steel in the region.

Animals. From children's organized sports on up through the professional ranks, we see teams named after animals. The animals are typically fierce, or at least feared, so that perhaps that association might attach itself to the team. Approximately half of the NFL's 32 teams are named after animals. The teams with potentially fear-inducing names are many, including the Chicago Bears, Cincinnati Bengals, Denver Broncos, Jacksonville Jaguars, and Carolina Panthers. However, a couple of NFL teams have a softer side—the Arizona Cardinals and the Miami Dolphins.

In college sports, there are a plethora of animals represented among the Division I programs. As in the professional ranks, the schools seem to strive for a fierce animal namesake, such as Tigers, which is shared by at least 13 schools, including Auburn University, Clemson University, Louisiana State University, and Grambling State University. Bears are also well represented by schools such as Brown University, Baylor University, and University of Maine (Black Bears). Still, other schools have opted for a more domesticated animal to represent their prowess on the field. Bulldogs hail from institutions such as University of Georgia, Mississippi State University, Gonzaga University and Yale University, while the Great Danes represent the University at Albany and Loyola University Maryland goes by the name Greyhounds. There are even at least four schools known as the Owls (Temple University, Rice University, Kennesaw State University and Florida Atlantic University), but only the University of California, Santa Cruz, uses a Banana Slug, a yellow slug indigenous to the area, as its mascot. Among college team names, however, it might be Evergreen State College that has the most unique name: the Geoducks (pronounced "GOO-ee-ducks"). This mollusk native to the Pacific Northwest is a burrowing clam that can live for 150 years.

People. Team names and nicknames might refer to people, their nationalities, ethnic heritage, religion, vocation or geographic personification. Some examples or teams with these types of names include the Notre Dame Fighting Irish and the Louisiana-Lafayette Ragin' Cajuns (ethnic heritage), Guilford College Quakers (religion), Texas A&M Corpus Christi Islanders, Mountaineers of Appalachian State University (geographic personification), and Purdue Boilermakers (vocation). Assorted human categories such as Pirates and Cowboys are also common staples for team names.

Whenever an organization adopts the name of an actual person as part of its brand identity, the concern is that the person continues to reflect the values of the brand. Over time, however, the perception of that person can change, and the change might also affect the perception of the brand's identity. Accordingly, naming an organizational asset after an actual person, particularly a living person, can sometimes prove to be problematic. For example, Nike removed Joe Paterno's name from its child care facility (formerly the Joe Paterno Child Development Center) after the iconic Penn State football coach was implicated in a massive child sex abuse scandal involving football coaching staff.

Potentially Divisive Names

A team's name is the centerpiece of its brand identity, and strategically speaking, should bring about positive connotations, yet the perception is subjective, so there is a potential negative side to the use of names that some may view as inappropriate or divisive. Divisive names may demean, defame, trivialize, dismiss, differentiate, marginalize, and ultimately diminish certain groups or individuals by perpetuating the inequities that may be reflected in larger society. Sport sociologist D. Stanley Eitzen (2016) identifies potentially problematic issues associated with brand identity elements that are racially insensitive or sexist in nature. Representative areas include three primary groupings: Native American, Confederate, and gender-biased/sexist imagery.

Redskins, Indians, Chiefs & Tribes. The issue of Native American names and imagery has spawned great debate over the past two decades. While some believe that the use of certain Native American imagery is respectful because it honors virtues such as strength, resourcefulness, and honor, various accounts to the contrary abound. Concern over stereotyped labels, the utilization of ethnic symbols, and the implementation of symbolism reflecting abusive, derogatory, or insensitive aspects associated with Native American and other indigenous groups should be an issue of importance and consideration, when relevant, for various stakeholders including athletes, coaches, administrators, educators, and other intended publics.

For example, notable professional, scholastic, and collegiate sport entities have been embroiled in controversy associated with the presence of Native American imagery. While some of these associations are more egregious than others, the hot button issues force administrative decisions and deliberations pertaining to policy and political considerations. Among the many notable examples are the Cleveland Indians, Atlanta Braves, Washington Redskins, Kansas City Chiefs, Florida State University Seminoles, etc.

Policy initiatives implemented by educational institutions (e.g., University of Wisconsin-Madison and the University of Minnesota), various school boards around the country, and other initiatives such as the NCAA's restrictions on hosting post-season play for teams with Native American imagery are all examples of issues associated with combating divisive imagery.

With regard to collegiate sport, the National Collegiate Athletic Association instituted a ban on higher education institutions that use offensive ("hostile or abusive") nicknames from hosting post-season play effective February 2006. Among the schools identified by this initiative were: University of North Dakota (Fighting Sioux), Arkansas State University (Indians), Central Michigan University (Chippewas), Florida State University (Seminoles), University of Illinois (Fighting Illini), University at Louisiana-Monroe (Indians), University of Utah (Utes), and the College of William & Mary (Tribe). Since that time, Florida State University, University of Utah, and Central Michigan appealed this decision and continued to utilize their Native American names, the University of Illinois board of trustees voted to retire the Chief Illiniwek name, image, and regalia, and Arkansas State University and the University of Louisiana at Monroe have each changed their team names from the Indians to the Red Wolves and Warhawks, respectively. The College of William & Mary was identified, in particular, by their feathered W&M logo, which has since been discontinued. In 2015, the University of North Dakota announced that they would be changing their team names from the Fighting Sioux to the Fighting Hawks.

Confederate Imagery. In addition to Native American imagery, Confederate imagery associated with sport can be divisive. The most noted example of Confederate sport imagery centers on the University of Mississippi, or Ole Miss. While Ole Miss has been mired in controversy because of its use of Confederate imagery, outside of Mississippi, other Southern states have also been embroiled in controversy. Although it's not a sport organization, the decades-long battle in South Carolina over the State House flying the confederate flag is a testament to the widespread controversy. Whether it is NCAA restrictions pertaining to hosting post-season play or former professional football player and college coach Steve Spurrier's vocal criticism of the flag's presence at the state capital, various concerns abound on the issue of using divisive names and imagery in sport.

The Confederate flag also has held a position of visibility within the world of NASCAR. Traditionally a Southern sport, NASCAR has long been viewed by many as being a sport that caters to "good old boys" and the South, although that is changing as NASCAR has grown in popularity in every area of the United States. Part of the Southern connotation has been associated not with the organization itself but with its fans and the presence of Confederate flags in unofficial NASCAR settings, namely tailgates (Lee, Bernthal, Whisenant & Mullane, 2010).

An interesting example of Confederate imagery tied to interscholastic sport was Nathan B. Forrest High School of Jacksonville, Florida. The school was named in 1959 after the Confederate general and first Grand Wizard of the Ku Klux Klan. The name and its teams, the Confederate Rebels, survived until 2014 when the school was renamed Westside High School and its teams became the Wolverines.

Gender-Biased/Sexist Imagery. Beyond issues of Native American and Confederate names and imagery, concern exists with regard to images that are perceived as gender-biased or sexist in nature. Eitzen (2016) identifies forms in which this occurs, including physical markers or qualifiers (pre-identifiers), which refers to adding "Lady" before a team name, viewing males as a false generic, and contrasting athletic names in a male/female polarity. Each of these characteristics is delineated below.

- *Physical markers:* names emphasize the physical appearance of women (e.g., the "Golden Girls" dance squad of the University of Missouri).
- *Adding the pre-identifier "Lady"* may evoke a connotation that is viewed as being distinctly inauthentic (e.g., "Lady Trojans" or "Lady Eagles") and sexist.
- Having names that present the male as a *false generic* provide a view where it is assumed that the masculine identifier represents the "norm" (e.g. NCAA Final Four/NCAA Women's Final Four) or oxymorons such as Rams or Gamecocks are representative of male animals that may inaccurately reflect a false generic name (e.g., a "Lady Ram" would be a "lady male sheep").
- *Male/female paired polarity* refers to groupings in which female teams may be viewed as being light hearted or cute (e.g., Wildcats/Wildkittens, Bears/Sugar Bears). Furthermore, there are additional examples that would be viewed as silly to many, such as pairing the Vikings with a corresponding female team with the name "ViQueens."

Miscellany. Additionally, team names and mascots may come in the form of the supernatural or imaginary (e.g., Drexel University Dragons), or the simply unique (the Fighting Artichokes of Scottsdale Community College or Minor League Baseball organizations such as Montgomery Biscuits, Jacksonville Jumbo Shrimp, and the Albuquerque Isotopes).

Just like the concern over divisive human imagery, there can also be concern over names that have supernatural references or are derived from religious beliefs. For example, certain religious organizations might take issue with organizations using names with "devils" or "demons" in them, although there are still many: Duke Blue Devils, Wake Forest Demon Deacons, and DePaul Blue Demons, to name a few.

Other schools or teams have a religious orientation and they intentionally draw on that in the naming of their sports teams because it comes from their very missions as religious institutions. Examples of these schools include Providence College Friars, Siena College Saints, and the North Greenville University Crusaders. On the professional level, there are the New Orleans Saints, Los Angeles Angels, and San Diego Padres.

Geographic Fit and Other Naming Considerations

At face value, some team names make much more sense (e.g., New England Patriots) than others (e.g., Utah Jazz). The NFL's New England Patriots have a name that is understandable to anyone with even a rudimentary understanding of American history because it draws upon the region's roots as the birthplace of the American Revolution. The Utah Jazz, however, has been left with a name that no longer reflects its history. While located in New Orleans, the Jazz moniker was a perfect fit because of the city's abundant connection with the musical style. There was no question that the "Jazz" moniker was reflective of the team's home city. When the team moved to Salt Lake City, however, it became known as the Utah Jazz. Salt Lake City is by no means a place that has been recognized for its deep connection to jazz music, which has resulted in an incongruent name for the team when taken at face value.

Decades after the Jazz left, New Orleans once again found itself home to an NBA franchise when the Charlotte Hornets relocated to the Mardi Gras City. Initially, the team retained the "Hornets" moniker, but it eventually decided to select a name that was more representative of the NOLA area. Ultimately, the Louisiana state bird, the pelican, became the inspiration for the new team name. Interestingly, not only did this decision lead to a new name for the New Orleans basketball franchise, but it also allowed the Hornets name to be reassumed by the Charlotte franchise in 2015 after determining that it would be a better organizational fit as compared to the previous Bobcats name.

Houston Dynamo. The Houston Dynamo was originally named the Houston 1836. Because the 1836 name was a nonconventional sport team name selection, it was quickly met with staunch objection. The impetus for the 1836 moniker was to signify the year that the City of Houston was founded. Unfortunately, 1836 also symbolized various points of objection from Mexican-American stakeholders. The vocal backlash from individuals and groups viewed the name as offensive from a historical perspective: Texas' independence from Mexico and the Battle of the Alamo. The resulting backlash, particularly from Latino citizens, resulted in swift disposal (just one month) of the short-lived 1836 name (Rein, Kotler & Shields, 2006).

Miami Marlins. The MLB's Miami Marlins team began playing in 1993 under the moniker "The Florida Marlins." This name was used by the organization from 1993 to 2011 when the team left their Miami Gardens home in Sun Life Stadium, located approximately 15 miles north of the city center and into the team's current palatial digs, Marlins Park. This $515-million stadium serves as a part of the Marlins' rebranding initiative that was meant to position the organization as Miami's team. Accordingly, the team chose a new name—the Miami Marlins—as well as new colors and logos. These moves aided in the team's goal to be more representative of their new hometown and its local faithful (Walsh & Lee, In Press).

Texas A&M. On the September 22, 2016, broadcast of *ESPN's College Gameday* program, there was a sign in the crowd that stated: "Texas A&M is the Auburn of Texas." While this sign was meant as a jab by an apparent Alabama Crimson Tide fan, there are various points of comparison for these institutions, and various other schools throughout the country. While Texas A&M and Auburn are both members of the West Division of the SEC, they are also both institutions noted for their contributions in the areas of agriculture and forestry. These schools, along with numbers of others throughout the country, are designated as "land-grant institutions." There are 76 land-grant institutions recognized by the

United States Department of Agriculture (USDA) (http://www.aplu.org/members/our-members/on-the-map/).

Each state has at least one designated land-grant institution, although some states have more than one. A number of these institutions either currently carry or have previously used the Agriculture & Mechanics (A&M) moniker. Many of the institutions also have state "flagship" university status. A state *flagship university* is a term applied to individual schools (sometimes specific campuses within a university system). Flagship universities are often the best-known institutions in the state, and such recognition could be due to factors such as being the first state institution to be established or being the largest (and perhaps most selective), or the status may be connected to the school's research-intensive profile.

State U. Each state has at least one state-funded university, and many states have multiple state-funded universities that bear the term "state" within the institutional moniker (e.g., Sam Houston State University, Murray State University). Other schools implement the "state" identifier by being the "state university" of a given state (e.g., North Dakota State University, North Carolina State University). Many of these universities are located in state capitals (e.g., Florida State University in Tallahassee, Georgia State University in Atlanta). While some schools proudly bear the "state" designation, others have opted to drop the "state" for branding purposes (e.g., Troy State University became Troy University; Memphis State University became University of Memphis).

Disney's ESPN Wide World of Sport Complex. After ESPN was acquired by Disney, the company saw a prime opportunity to leverage the sports giant—the "Worldwide Leader in Sports"—to promote its Wide World of Sports complex in Central Florida. Capitalizing on the opportunity to diversify its entertainment offerings by rebranding the complex, Disney was able to leverage both brands and the connection to Disney World as "the happiest place on earth." As both the Disney and ESPN brands are leaders in their respective industries, the transformed complex benefited from unparalleled brand synergy (Lee, Gregg, Miloch & Pursglove, In Press).

Baseball's Never Been Yummier. On November 2, 2016, the Jacksonville Suns announced that the Minor League baseball team had changed its name to the Jacksonville Jumbo Shrimp. The unique name selection sent reverberations through social media and news comment boards. The hashtag "#JumboShrimp" was instantly trending and Jacksonville citizens, sports fans, and those interested in team names and logos were quick to chime in. Comment sections were replete with quips relating to the silliness of the name and the diminutive size of the sea creature, and there were plenty of comparisons to other sport properties and their names—both good and bad. This included references to the team's league—the Southern League—which is a Double AA classification of Minor League Baseball (MiLB). As of the time of the Jumbo Shrimp announcement, the Southern League included aquatic creatures such as the Shuckers out of Biloxi, Mississippi; the Blue Wahoos of Pensacola, Florida; and now Jumbo Shrimp. These teams complement the taste palette of the league that already hosts the Montgomery Biscuits.

Along with the announcement of the new name, other organizational brand identity elements were presented, including new logos and uniforms. The Jumbo Shrimp also need a new tagline, as the Suns had long used the tagline "Baseball's never been Hotter [than the Jacksonville Suns]." Perhaps the new tagline will be replaced with something more palatable (pun intended).

Who Are U? Public universities named after their geographic location are particularly susceptible to shorthanding because their formal names tend to be long and sometimes cumbersome. This shorthanding may lead to confusion when the loyal followers of one school's team venture closer to the territory of another. For example, the "U of M" might perfectly differentiate the University of Minnesota from a local private university in Minneapolis, but that is not the case if the audience is not a local one. To a broader audience, "U of M" could refer to the University of Michigan, the University of Memphis or the University of Maryland, among many others.

Other aspects associated with abbreviated names extends to the professional sports ranks, where the formal names of many teams are often shorthanded by the people who follow them. For example, consider the Boston Red Sox: local fans never use the full name; they simply refer to the team as the Red Sox or even just the Sox. Local media use a different shorthand. To save space and time, the Boston Red Sox may become the BoSox.

Which Carolina? Depending on which of the Carolinas you're in, you might think a reference to "Carolina" refers to the University of North Carolina at Chapel Hill or the University of South Carolina in Columbia. Both schools share the "Carolina" nickname, even though being just a four-hour drive and slightly more than 200 miles apart causes confusion among Carolinians and fans alike. The schools have widely divergent color palettes, and it seems they are willing to endure any potential nickname confusion because both universities also claim a trademark in the term "Carolina."

USC East or USC West? As with the Carolina nicknames, the University of South Carolina also shares a confusing acronym shorthand with the University of Southern California. Both schools shorthand their long names to simply "USC." While this is likely not a problem for fans and students given the geographic distance between the two schools and the fact that their teams play in different athletic conferences, the two universities also share a variation of the color "maroon" in their color palettes. The University of South Carolina's signature color is Garnet and the University of Southern California has Cardinal.

(Wo)Men of Troy. USC (University of Southern California) was also involved in an institutional brand identity/intellectual property disagreement with Troy University. USC sent a cease and desist letter to Troy University to inform the state university in Alabama that it was not to use the phrase "Men of Troy." The "Men of Troy" moniker was utilized in several ways by the Troy University athletic program, which is known as the Trojans. USC also goes by the Trojans moniker and has used references to the Men of Troy and Women of Troy.

University of North Florida: "UNF" or "North Florida." UNF, like many schools, has debated the best name. According to the university's brand identity standards, university representatives can refer to the school as the "University of North Florida" or "UNF," but not "North Florida." However, the university athletic department has opted to promote the "North Florida" moniker as it is viewed as serving purposes of identifiability and recognition (e.g., a viewer watching the ticker on ESPN may not have a clue what UNF is, but North Florida, or even "N. Florida," is more identifiable). Schools that may not be well known on a regional or national scale should look at challenges and considerations such as this. In the case of the University of North Florida, it should be noted that this reality has resulted in the athletic department being given the opportunity—at least temporarily—to deviate from the school's brand identity guidelines.

Unique Pronunciations. Another consideration when it comes to naming is the reality that sport teams and organizations may have pronunciations that deviate from common usage. For example, the North Dakota State University Bison is actually pronounced *Bi-Zun.* Another interesting example is found in the storied college football stadium Jordan-Hare Stadium, home to the Auburn Tigers. The name of the location is pronounced "Jurdan" rather than "JOR-dan," which is a common pronunciation of that surname. An additional example of unique naming considerations can be found in the common misused or mispronounced reference to certain sport entities. A classic example of this is how many people commonly pronounce Clemson University as if it had a "p" in the name—"CLEMP-son."

Things Do Not Always Add Up. Naming anomalies sometimes affect geographic and even numerical fit when it comes to the team's athletic conference. For example, the Atlanta Braves were known as "America's Team" during the 1980s and enjoyed national broadcasts on *Superstation WTBS*. The Georgia franchise was a member of the National League West even though the franchise was one of the east-most teams playing in MLB. While time, expansion, and league realignment rectify that issue, as the team currently plays in the NL East, there are still misnomers associated with geographic identification of teams. For example, the Nashville Predators play in the Western Conference of the NHL and the New Orleans Pelicans play in the Western Conference of the NBA, despite clearly being in the Eastern portion of the United States.

In the world of intercollegiate sport, conference names do not always reflect the geographic fit of some of the conference's member institutions. Consider that the following schools are currently members of the *Big East*: Butler (IN), Creighton (NE), Marquette (WI), DePaul (IL), and Xavier (OH). Furthermore, geographical anomalies are not the only misfit names that can exist. Conference expansion and realignment have wreaked havoc on the numbers associated with certain conferences. For example, as of this writing, the *Big 12* has 10 schools and the *Big 10* has 14 schools.

Collegiate "Sand Volleyball." The sport of collegiate beach volleyball presents various significant marketing issues. The relatively new sport of collegiate beach volleyball has many attractive elements, including "place of sport" issues such as sportscape factors and atmospherics, the brand appeal of the sport, and even uniform considerations. One interesting marketing consideration was the decision to initially go with the "sand volleyball" moniker. As names are key, this terminology was chosen to be a more inclusive term for the population of schools under the NCAA umbrella, which represents geographic regions that are not in close proximity to the ocean. Ultimately, after years of using the sand volleyball name, the NCAA eventually opted to use the more widely regarded moniker "beach volleyball."

Conclusion

Names are chief components in an organization's overall brand identity portfolio. This chapter discussed assorted considerations and conventions associated with various types of names within the sport industry. Names carry great weight and meaning, and as such, organizations need to be mindful when choosing names to select both meaningful and appropriate monikers for both the short- and long-term.

Chapter 2

Logos and Mascots

Logos are graphic designs—whether symbols or logotypes—used by organizations primarily for identification (Alessandri, 2009; Henderson & Cote, 1998; Lee, 2011a). An organization's logo may appear alongside or without the organization's name, depending on the notoriety of the brand and the history of the logo, but either way, the design serves as a vital communication asset as it becomes a de facto organizational brand "signature" (Wheeler, 2006). The decision to use a purely graphic logo or a simple logotype is dependent upon the image the organization would like to cultivate in the minds of fans and the public, but Henderson and Cote (1998) advocate developing a logo with some familiar meaning, as this improves recognition and consensus among those who view the logo. Because the efficacy of brand identity to help consumers form associations lies in classical conditioning, the key to successfully exploiting either an iconic logo or a logotype is consistency in its promotion. Over time, the public "learns" positive or negative associations based on their experiences with it.

Consistent and regular promotion of a brand identity, and in this case the logo, will aid in association formation, and ultimately in achieving the desired image. Inconsistent promotion—either by neglecting to use the logo in consistent colors across media or by neglecting to use the logo on all appropriate touchpoints—could result in a delay in association formation (Alessandri, 2001).

An organization often dedicates substantial financial and human resources to the development and promotion of its logo in its quest to build greater awareness, generate recognition, or enhance the organization's image (Henderson & Cote, 1998). Over time, however, even the best logos are modified by organizations to reflect changes in cultural norms, service delivery or current trends. Some organizations will make dramatic changes in their logos, but smaller changes over time reflect a "migration" in the logo design since rarely does one design withstand decades without some need for updating. Logo changes may be made for a variety of reasons, such as to align with large or small organizational changes, but they should never be undertaken on a whim. To change a logo that is otherwise performing well would represent a disruption in association formation.

Henderson and Cote (1998) identified three specific attributes that can enhance an organization's logo: elaboration, naturalness, and harmony. Elaboration denotes the richness of the design, which is comprised of depth, activeness, and complexity (Henderson & Cote, 1998). For a logo design, depth signifies the extent that a logo includes a three-dimensional appearance. The complexity of a design refers to aspects such as intricacy and the ability of the design to capture the essence of the organizational message. A logo's activeness refers to its focus on brand dimensions, which convey motion or flow for the logo. Montgomery College, a Division III college in Maryland, is home to the Raptors. Logo elaboration is well represented in the college's use of one logo that depicts a fierce raptor seemingly in flight while simultaneously "skidding" to a half with its talons outstretched. Viewing the logo, there is no mistaking the intended message that Montgomery College is a program that considers itself aggressive and competitive.

Another significant characteristic of a logo is the concept of naturalness, which suggests that the design depicts commonly experienced objects (Henderson & Cote, 1998). In other words, can the logo be described organically or through representative attributes of the design? Representativeness reflects the realism in the design.

The opposite of realism is abstract. Abstract logos could refer to logos in which observers would have no (or limited) information regarding the image provided. Henderson and Cote (1998) recommend the use of representative logos more than abstract ones due to a greater aptitude for understandability. They also recommend the use of organic designs composed of natural shapes, rather than geometric designs that are apt to be angular and more abstract, as organic or natural shapes may be more meaningful (Henderson & Cote, 1998). Perhaps the best logo to illustrate this characteristic is the logo employed by the Stanford Cardinal: California's historic El Palo Alto tree in the forefront with a large "Block S" in the signature Cardinal color behind.

Finally, Henderson and Cote (1998) posit that logos with symmetry and balance create a harmonious image. Having elements that are identical on both sides of the image's axis creates symmetry, and balance refers to having an equal division of weight on either side of the logo. In other words, both sides of the logo appear "even" to the casual eye and do not look weighted toward one side disproportionately. Harvard University athletics employs a perfectly balanced logo: a crimson shield with a white "Block H" in the center. If an imaginary line were drawn down the middle, each side would be perfectly symmetrical.

Logotypes and Wordmarks

Logotypes and wordmarks can take the place of a symbol-based logo to serve as a primary identifier, and typography itself can serve as a marketing communication tool. Accordingly, the selection of an appropriate font is vital for generating the preferred stakeholder responses (Hussain & Ferdous, 2015). The typeface must be distinctive enough that, even in isolation, the typeface is associated with the brand. In sport, there is a myriad of teams and organizations using logotypes as either primary or secondary identifiers.

The Boston Red Sox employ a primary identifier that is two red socks with white toes and white heels against a baseball, but the socks and baseball are accompanied in a larger outside circle with the words "Boston Red Sox" in a truly distinctive typeface. The red sock with the white heel and toe is often used in isolation, as is the distinctive Red Sox alphabet logotype. The typeface, known as Bosox, stands alone to competently identify the team. In fact, players wear hats with a simple Bosox "B," and fans everywhere wear t-shirts with Boston Red Sox written in the Bosox font.

Other institutions, instead of having an entire alphabet, employ a distinctive wordmark that is just a letter or two (or maybe even three). The New York Yankees, with the interlocking "NY," are an example of this, as are the Cincinnati Bengals, with the orange tiger-striped "B." University athletic programs that employ one letter as their brand identity include Syracuse University, the University of Michigan, Michigan State University, and the University of Tennessee.

MSU Baseball. The Mississippi State University Bulldogs baseball program employs a stacked "MS" logo. The MS logo that adorns the baseball team's hats is used only for the school's baseball program, and it is considered an honor to earn the right to wear it. The significance of the exclusive athletic mark was detailed in the ESPN-produced *SEC Storied* documentary *Thunder & Lightning*, which chronicled the history of the Mississippi State University baseball program and its legendary former stars, Will Clark and Rafael Palmeiro.

The Scarlet (red) ... err, Crimson ... err, Cardinal Letter: Numerous notable sport organizations utilize a stylistic letter "A." The University of Alabama (Crimson), University of Arkansas (Cardinal), and the MLB's Atlanta Braves (Scarlet Red) all implement a script A that have high levels of similarity.

Crests/Seals/Emblems. Official seals used as organizational identifiers are typically rooted in the history of an organization—particularly educational institutions—and are usually reserved for serious or official purposes as a mark of guarantee, such as for academic transcripts, diplomas, and official documents and contracts. Before technology made it simple to produce even the most complex designs, seals were designed to be more complicated to prevent misappropriation (Lee, Cavanaugh & Alessandri, In Press). Observers of an educational institution's official seal might find elements of that seal in the athletic department's brand identity. Stanford University, for example, uses the El Palo Alto tree in both its official seal and its athletic department logo.

The Example of the Fleur-de-lis. The fleur-de-lis is a popular symbol found on everything from jewelry to furniture. The fleur-de-lis is also commonly used in sport settings as part of brand identity, particularly sport organizations in the state of Louisiana. The NFL's New Orleans Saints have long served as a symbol of New Orleans, the state of Louisiana generally, and even surrounding areas along the Gulf Coast. As such, the team and its fan base regularly tout symbolic affiliations: displaying the black and gold team colors, signs, chants, and stickers that read "Geaux Saints," shouting the team chant "Who Dat," playing the old hymn *When the Saints Go Marching In,* and, of course, displaying the iconic fleur-de-lis symbol (Lee, 2011c).

NOLA residents and sport fans also recognize the fleur-de-lis symbol in various other sport organizations, including the NBA's New Orleans Pelicans (as well as the former New Orleans Hornets, who used a "fleur-de-bee" logo) and college programs, where the symbol is a primary identifier of the University of Louisiana-Lafayette and its Ragin' Cajun athletic program and has also been adopted in various forms by the state's flagship university, Louisiana State University (LSU) (Lee, 2011c).

Mascots

What Are Mascots? "Mascots are visible associations as they provide a means of 'community' for regional, national, and international sport groups; school-based athletic programs; professional sport organizations; and non-sport entities alike" (Lee, 2011b, p. 867). Mascots serve as pseudo-living representations (such as a person, animal, or object) of a brand that become part of the culture associated with their respective organizations. The roles and functions of mascots are multidimensional, as they serve as institutional totems or symbolic representations, and may represent, endorse, entertain, and even prompt people to action (Lee, 2011b). Over time, many mascots become iconic, adding to the lore of the organizations they represent. In the world of collegiate sport, mascots such as Sparty the Spartan at Michigan State University and the University of Georgia's Uga and Hairy Dawg are vivid examples that resonate with institutional stakeholders. A prime corporate example is the Chick-fil-A cows who have been utilized in various company marketing initiatives ranging from national advertising campaigns to sponsoring school and local community events (Cianfrone, Tranova & Lee, 2017).

Mascots may be human or humanized, adding a further connection to those who are impacted by them. For example, when the University of Evansville decided to develop a new Ace Purple mascot, the school rebranding initiative provided not only a new costume for the human acting as the mascot, but it also included graphic mascot images for use in a variety of marketing efforts.

Though the aforementioned positive associations can bring about desirable organizational goals, there are also areas of concern associated with the use of mascots. Some mascots have proven to be divisive brand identity symbols that demean, trivialize, marginalize, and ultimately diminish certain groups or individuals (Eitzen, 2016). These include symbols that may be racially insensitive or sexist in nature. According to Eitzen (2016), just as with team names, divisive images can typically be classified into three primary groups: Native American imagery, Confederate imagery, and gender-biased/sexist imagery. In addition to these classifications, there are other divisive mascots that schools, particularly public high schools, have chosen to keep, regardless of the controversy surrounding them. Examples of these include the Yuma Criminals in Arizona, as well as the Freeburg Community High School Midgets and the Centralia Orphans in Illinois (Alessandri & Lee, 2016).

Physical Mascots. Physical mascots occur in a variety of forms, including people in costumes occurring as both "regular" people (e.g., West Virginia Mountaineer), costumed characters (e.g., Sparty the Spartan at Michigan State), people in animal costumes (e.g., Jaxson De Ville of the Jacksonville Jaguars or the San Diego Chicken), and live animals (e.g., Bevo at the University of Texas).

The use of live animals provides a great identifier and rally point for sport programs. For example, notable collegiate animal mascots include Mike the Tiger (LSU), Ralphie (the buffalo at the University of Colorado), Ramses the ram—complete with horns painted light blue—at the University of North Carolina at Chapel Hill, and Uga X, the University of Georgia's bulldog, and many other iconic totems of pride, identification, and inspiration.

Mascots in Action. Many animals and people have well-known game day exploits that have become notable brand identity touchpoints in the world of sport. Iconic actions occurring in collegiate football include the running of Sooner Schooner at Oklahoma, the pre-game ritual of Chief Osceola and Renegade at Florida State, the War Eagle Flight at Auburn, and Ralphie's Run at the University of Colorado.[1]

Beyond these, a number of campuses serve as home to their iconic live animal mascots, where their presence, and their living quarters, serve as campus destinations for students, fans, and other visitors who would like to visit the beloved inhabitants.

Stetson: Mad Hatter → John B. Stetson. When Stetson University underwent its most recent brand identity change, the school added multiple new sports and added important brand identity elements, one of which was the newly developed mascot "John B." The new John B. replaced the previous mascot, the "Mad Hatter." The Mad Hatter had a wild hairstyle and large teeth and its appearance raised concerns about scaring children (Lee, Wilson & Gregg, In Press). Because of his potential for frightening young fans, the Mad Hatter avoided public appearances for years prior to the unveiling of the new John B. mascot. The new mascot was developed through a "Mascot Challenge" posed to alumni, students, faculty, staff, and university associated organizations. Eventually, more than 70 submissions were received by a committee consisting of stakeholders from the Stetson University athletics department, alumni, and community, as well as from Disney's character division. John B., the winning mascot, was a nod to the university's

1. Interestingly, Colorado football's twitter handle is @RunRalphieRun

founder, hat manufacturer John B. Stetson. At the announcement of the new mascot, Stetson University Athletic Director Jeff Altier stated, "John B. represents the University's heritage and embraces the traditions that are so important to our students and alumni" ("John B.," 2012).

New SLU Billiken. Saint Louis University carries the unique name and mascot of the Billikens. The school embarked on a major athletic rebranding initiative in 2015, part of which included the development of a new mascot. The new Billiken mascot sports the look of the updated Billiken logo, which was revealed during a special event between the women's and men's soccer teams in Robert R. Hermann Stadium on September 20, 2016 ("New Billiken Mascot Makes Debut," 2016). Various St. Louis area sports mascots, including Louie (from the NHL's St. Louis Blues), Ruffy (the Frontier League's River City Rascals), Izzy (the Frontier League's Gateway Grizzlies) and Bushwhacker (the Major Arena Soccer League's St. Louis Ambush) attended this event to usher in the latest member of the St. Louis mascot fraternity.

Though the new mascot was ushered in with great pageantry, the Billiken fanfare was met with a resounding thud. The new mascot was not well received and resulted in a national narrative that panned the creepy mascot. The sentiment was addressed by *Sports Illustrated,* which published an online article entitled "Saint Louis University has a new mascot and it's absolutely terrifying" (Gartland, 2016). The school responded to the negative attention by quickly pulling the new mascot and ultimately revealing plans to develop a new, less controversial one.

Logoed Mascots (Cartoon Images)

Ace Purple. The University of Evansville is home to the unique mascot named Ace Purple. Formerly the Pioneers, the new Ace Purple represented a caricature of a riverboat gambler. The original Ace Purple smoked cigars, carried a gun, and toted a club with a spike on the end (Gregg, Pierce, Lee, Himstedt & Felver, 2013). The negative associations with images of gambling, violence, and the image of the riverboat gambler proved to be problematic for the university. Keith Butz, the creator of Purdue Boilermaker's Purdue Pete, was tasked with crafting a mascot that personified the desired traits of cunning, daring, and quick-wittedness (Gregg et al., 2013).

Aside from the physical mascot, the Evansville athletic department elected to eventually redesign their Ace Purple (cartoon) logo. The old logo featured a mustachioed riverboat gambler, wearing a cap with an ace of spades peeking out of his hat band (Gregg et al., 2013). The new Ace Purple was more refined and debonair. The cartooned logo image of Ace Purple is also versatile in that it has been employed across various university marketing touchpoints, both digitally and in print.

The Varied Mascots of the Montgomery Biscuits. The Montgomery Biscuits, the AA Southern League affiliate of the Tampa Bay Rays, are a unique sport organization, with an even more unique brand identity. Aside from the unusual "Biscuits" moniker, the team has also used assorted mascots to connect to their fans and other desired audiences. This includes Big Mo, Monty, and Miss Gravy. Big Mo is the "big, orange, fuzzy, biscuit-loving beast" that serves as the organization's costumed mascot (Lee & Mathner, In Press). The Biscuits also use the cartoon logo mascot Monty, an anthropomorphized biscuit that features a pat of butter for its tongue. Additionally, following the contest to name the newest member of the Montgomery Biscuits mascot family, the pot-bellied pig was subsequently named "Miss Gravy" (officially "Miss Gravy The Duchess of Pork"). While this latest mascot was a further testament to the organization's willingness to take a risk and be creative with its brand identity, the mascot was discontinued just a couple of seasons later.

Conclusion

This chapter discussed the myriad characteristics associated with logos and mascots in a variety of sport industries (from high school through the professional ranks). This includes notable examples and further discussions of noteworthy—and some notorious—logos and mascots. In sport, logos and mascots serve as notable totems and strong identifiers for the organizations they represent. Mascots come in a variety of forms, including people in set attire, people in various costumes, and animals. Furthermore, mascots may also be presented in cartoon (logo) forms, which allow for versatility in print and digital formats.

Chapter 3

Color

Every organized team in sport, from the amateur through professional ranks, has long been aware of the relative ease of associating themselves with a color. Many organizations have a signature color: that one color that is so clearly and closely linked to that organization that it is undeniably representative of only that organization. Fans at every level can identify with the team simply by wearing its signature color. In sport, color choice has most often been determined far in the past, and the color—or colors—is often linked to that particular organization's traditions. Many sport organizations have a color palette: a collection of colors that is regularly used to represent the team or organization in question.

Research shows that color can reflect a certain mood or feeling. In the sport context, color can become a strong singular identifier if the color is unique, or a combination of colors can very quickly identify a team. In both cases, the color becomes another brand identity element that can foster positive associations. Just picture a college football stadium on game day: a sea of color to support a favored team.

Holtzschue (2006) writes regarding color theory: "Color is stimulating, calming, expressive, disturbing, impressional [sic], cultural, exuberant, symbolic. It pervades every aspect of our lives ...

good color can determine [a product's] success or failure in the consumer market … color means business" (p. 2).

Holtzschue (2006) refers to color theory as two-pronged. It is the convergence of the quest for a color-order system and the search for harmony in color combinations. On a practical level, the study of color focuses on three areas: learning to distinguish the many qualities of different colors, learning to understand the "instability" of color—given that colors appear differently depending on the light, where they are placed relative to other colors, and in which medium they are placed—and learning to develop consistently effective color combinations (Holtzschue, 2006).

University color palettes are customarily comprised of representative primary and secondary colors, and very often tertiary colors depending on the specific application. Color has the power to make a brand touchpoint more interesting and can reinforce the meaning in a design, but colors should be easy to process at a glance. Specifically, Itten (1997) recommends the use of five or fewer colors.

However many colors are contained in the color palette, it is imperative that the colors are used consistently across brand identity touchpoints. The institution's primary colors serve as the dominant colors, while secondary colors are used to complement the others and convey a specific message (Hynes, 2009; Wheeler, 2006).

Generally speaking, colors have commonly associated meanings. Purple is associated with royalty and white with purity, etc., but universities typically have a long legacy associated with their colors, and many have come to associate more literal meanings with their colors. For example, the University of North Carolina at Chapel Hill traces its use of "Carolina Blue" back to the 1800s, when students were required to be a member of one of two literary societies—one society's color was baby blue and the other was white (University Colors, 2014).

In 1995, the Supreme Court provided all organizations with an additional legal way to protect their brand identities when it ruled that color alone could be registered as a trademark (Qualitex, 514 U.S. 159). While sport organizations and teams of all kinds have used color as a part of their marketing mix for decades, never before was there the opportunity to "own" a color, both figuratively and literally, and thereby profit from the promotion of it.

"Bleeding" Color. Many college sports fans will say they "bleed" a particular color, using the metaphor to lay claim to their status as diehard fans. Sometimes being a fan of one team automatically disqualifies those fans from wearing a rival's color. For example, Florida State University Seminoles fans may say they "bleed garnet and gold," while simultaneously, those same fans might refuse at all times to wear "orange and blue" as those are the colors of the rival University of Florida Gators. Also, consider the extreme example at Stephen F. Austin State University. Students are not supposed to wear the color orange on campus because that is the signature color of their in-state rival, Sam Houston State University.

De Facto Colors. Louisiana State University adopted purple and gold in 1893. Legend has it that the football coach and some players were looking for something to liven up the team's dull gray jerseys. The local craft store they visited was stocking up for the Carnival season (which ends on Fat Tuesday with Mardi Gras) and had plenty of purple and gold ribbon. The team bought all the store had, made some ornaments for the jerseys and had unofficially developed the university's new color palette (Theriot, 2014). Even with a strong dual-color palette, however, the purple is a stronger singular identifier and most definitely the university's signature color.

Other teams, most notably in college athletics, have signature colors reflected in their team names. Among these are the Harvard Crimson, the Delaware Blue Hens, and the Dartmouth Big Green.

With a seemingly limited supply of colors available, or at least clearly discernible shades for marketing purposes, it is incumbent on an organization to use the exact color it has identified as its signature color. This is where Holtzschue's so-called "business of color" plays a role. Commercial color-order systems provide efficiency and consistency to the design process. Specifically, the Pantone Matching System (PMS) is one of the most widely used commercial color-order systems. It provides "a palette of standardized colors for a wide range of products, ranging from printer inks to software, color films, plastics, and markers" (p. 8). Each of the colors has a unique identification number that corresponds to a formula for mixing the proper inks to make that color; graphic designers use the PMS swatch books during the design phase to ensure color consistency.

Using PMS numbers ensures color consistency across media and over time, but it also simplifies the process of working with outside designers and vendors because PMS numbers are universal, thereby eliminating any confusion between the organization and the vendor or designer regarding a color's hue or shade.

While PMS numbers ensure that the color used is the organization's signature color, it is possible that more than one organization uses the same PMS color. While the concept of brand identity centers on developing a unique overall "look and feel" for a brand, when it comes to color palettes, there is naturally going to be some overlap. The Boston Red Sox and New York Yankees share a fierce and storied rivalry, and fans on either side may be loath to admit they have anything in common. But they do—color. When they each wear their team's signature "Red Sox blue" and "Yankee blue" colors, they are both actually wearing PMS 289. Fans of six other teams in Major League Baseball are also wearing the same dark blue (Korkidis, 2012).

Meanings of Colors

The use of color can provide multiple connection points as well as sources of identification and meaning. Even basic colors combined in a creative way convey a deeper meaning. For example, there are multiple meanings contained in the Olympic Rings logo. According to the Olympic Museum (2007):

> The five rings represent the five continents. They are interlaced to show the universality of Olympism and the meeting of the athletes of the world during the Olympic Games. On the Olympic flag, the rings appear on a white background. Combined in this way, the six colours [sic] of the flag (blue, yellow, black, green, red and white) rep-

resent all nations. It is a misconception, therefore, to believe that each of the colours [sic] corresponds to a certain continent. (p. 3)

Symbolically, colors that have long been associated with sport organizations take on particular associations that foster positive connotations with those organizations, but long before those organizational specific associations, those colors had common associations. Table 3 outlines several primary and secondary colors along with their common associations.

Table 3: The Meaning of Colors

Color	Common Associations
Blue	Trustworthy; dependable; secure
Red	Aggressive; energetic; provocative
Green	Health; freshness; prestige
Orange	Exuberance; fun, vitality
Purple	Sophistication; royalty; mystery
Black	Bold; powerful; classic
White	Simplicity; cleanliness; purity

Source: Williams, J. (2007). "Your Brand's True Colors" Retrieved from https://www.entrepreneur.com/article/175428

Color Palettes

Many organizational colors are complementary, meaning that the colors are located on opposite sides of the color wheel. These complementary colors typically have good comparison and contrast and are generally found pleasing to the eye. Louisiana State University utilizes the color scheme of purple and gold. They employ an oppositional color scheme using the complementary colors of purple and gold (yellow). Another Louisiana School, Mc-

Neese State, uses a (royal) blue and yellow (sunflower gold) color palette.

Other schools may take a non-traditional—and non-complementary—approach to their color palettes. The University of Wyoming, for example, utilizes a traditional logo that is representative of the state symbol of the cowboy (or cowgirl), but the university chose a color palette of three simple colors: brown, white and gold. It makes for a distinctive look, and it is a color palette that is not used very often and not by any other major intercollegiate athletic program. While the color palette does offer distinctiveness, it goes against traditional branding logic rooted in traditional color theory. Similarly, the Virginia Tech Hokies employ and embrace a color palette that includes maroon and orange. This makes the Hokies unique in their choice since they are the only major program to utilize this color combination.

Red, White, and Blue. In the United States, the patriotic color palette of red, white and blue is employed by the American teams in countless high-profile international sporting events (e.g., Olympic Games, World Cup men's and women's soccer, the Ryder Cup USA team) as well as a variety of professional sports: Atlanta Braves (MLB), Houston Texans (NFL), Philadelphia 76ers (NBA), New York Rangers (NHL), New England Revolution (MLS), Boston Red Sox (MLB), and New England Patriots (NFL). There are also various college teams that use red, white, and blue, such as Ole Miss, Southern Methodist University, University of Kansas, Louisiana Tech, Robert Morris University, and the University of South Alabama, to name a few.

"How Blue Are You?"

Carolina Blue. Baby blue is a unique color choice for a college athletic program, but it has invoked tremendous loyalty. Some fans might refuse at all times to wear "Prussian blue," the official color of the school's primary rival, Duke University (Lee, Cavanagh & Alessandri, In Press).

Petty Blue. Richard Petty left an indelible footprint on the world of NASCAR and has become an iconic figure in sport. Petty was noted for his famed #43 car (which was also noted for its long-running association with sponsor STP), and the color that has gone on to be known as "Petty Blue." As legend has it, the color was developed from a dilemma in which blue paint was needed, but there was not enough available. The remaining blue paint was mixed with white, and ultimately a signature hue and symbol were born (Lee & Whisenant, 2011).

Pittsburgh Is a Black and Yellow Town. Pittsburgh sports fans know the city is famous for its synchronicity of colors across its professional sports teams: specifically, its black and yellow color palette. The three major professional sport franchises in the city, the Pittsburgh Pirates (MLB), Steelers (NFL), and Penguins all use the black and yellow color palette. The Penguins were the last to adopt the color palette and did so to fall in line with the "colors of Pittsburgh." Musician Wiz Khalifa is noted for his song "Black and Yellow," which pays homage to his hometown and the hometown team colors.

Silver and Black Attack: Raiders. The silver and black color palette sends a strong message. This iconic color combination has been used by various sport organizations, perhaps most notably by the NFL's Oakland Raiders and the NBA's San Antonio Spurs. The silver and black of the Raiders were eventually adopted by the NHL's Los Angeles Kings. These teams and their colors became a pronounced fashion statement in the early 1990s when youth and adults across the country started wearing Starter jackets and hats in this color palette. The ESPN 30 for 30 film *Straight Outta LA* details this cultural phenomenon.

"Purple Reigns." While most teams and schools enlist the use of traditional color palettes (e.g., red and blue; blue and gold), many sport entities implement the color purple. While traditional color theory posits that the color purple conveys associations of sophistication, royalty, and mystery, the use of purple also has the benefit of standing out among a sea of similarly colored athletic teams. Among the schools that employ a shade of purple as a signature color: the University of Evansville, University of Washington, Louisiana State University, Kansas State University, James Madison University, Texas Christian University, Furman University, Northwestern University, Stephen F. Austin State University, St. Michael's College, and East Carolina University.

"Orange You Glad You Stand Out?" Much like the aforementioned school using purple as a signature color, the color orange is a striking color that various universities have used as part of their brand identities, including Oregon State University, Oklahoma State University, Syracuse University, Sam Houston State University, University of Tennessee, and Mercer University, among others. Assorted other schools such as the University of Florida, Boise State University, University of Illinois, and the University of Virginia implement an orange and blue color scheme. Other universities use orange alongside an additional color: Clemson University (purple and orange) and Virginia Tech (orange and maroon). The University of Texas utilizes a burnt orange as its primary color.

In the Pink. The color pink has become a popular color in sport during the month of October because many sport organizations align themselves with breast cancer research and advocacy organizations, but also generally to presumably appeal to a female demographic when it comes to selling equipment (e.g., golf balls, softball bats) and merchandise. Pink is also used less pragmatically and more symbolically in sport settings. A classic example was former University of Iowa Hawkeye football coach Hayden Fry's use of pink in the opposing team's locker rooms. Legend has it that Frye used his background in psychology to serve the purpose of both emasculating opposing teams while using pink for its calming effect.

Pink and Black. Even unusual pairings such as pink and black are found in professional sports. A classic example of this was the use of the colors by professional wrestling legend Bret "The Hitman" Hart. Hart and his wrestling family made the iconic color scheme a strong brand identifier by using the pair of colors for television programs, live action events, video games, and merchandise. The Hitman moniker was also used as the namesake for the Calgary Hitmen, a major junior ice hockey team based in Calgary, Alberta, Canada. Though the team no longer employs this color palette, its name and original colors were based on the wrestling star and Canada's national icon.

October + Pink = "Pinktober." As mentioned above, the color pink has also been used in sport for various cause-related marketing (CRM) practices as part of organizations' corporate social responsibility (CSR) activities. For example, October is designated by the National Breast Cancer Foundation, Inc. as Breast Cancer Awareness Month. As such, sport organizations have partnered with organizations such as the Susan G. Komen for the Cure. The infusing of the color pink into sport settings ranges from pink penalty flags in the NFL, to uniform and equipment modification in the MLB, to even changing the color of the ring ropes to pink in the WWE during October (sometimes identified as "Pinktober").

While much good can come from such associations, there has been concern regarding the over-commercialization of some pink cause initiatives. The term "Pinkwashing" has been used to describe the practice of merely using the pink ribbon symbol as a means to market products in a context that may be more profit oriented than cause-centered. The documentary *Pink Ribbons, Inc.* analyzed such practices while examining commercialization and philanthropic motives and practices associated with the presence of pink ribbons.

"Camouflage Culture" is a term used to describe locations and settings where camouflage is likely to be prevalent. Camouflage is a coloration pattern that uses a combination of colors, shading and other attributes to develop a pattern that is often employed to make an object hard to see or to disguise it as something it isn't. In 1986, Mossy Oak's founder and CEO, Toxey Haas, gathered up leaves, branches, sticks, bark, dirt and grass, and took his bags of nature into a local textile manufacturer to make camouflage hunting apparel: realistic images and patterns of the woods on fabric (Forsyth, In Press).

Camouflage is able to serve a variety of purposes on an assortment of products, both without the sport industry and without. Camouflage attire can be worn by hunters and outdoor enthusiasts to blend into nature, and some may simply like the look of camouflage and choose to wear it as a fashion statement. Individuals such as Larry the Cable Guy, the cast of Duck Dynasty, and many others fit that bill. A variety of sport organizations from collegiate athletics and the professional leagues have embraced the camouflage culture by offering everything from t-shirts to hats and athletic pants.

Beyond clothing products, camouflage patterns by Realtree and Mossy Oak have used camouflage to adorn a seemingly endless line of products, from duct tape to table lamps to pick-up trucks. The Mossy Oak company has a simple licensing and merchandising equation: partner's quality product(s) + Mossy Oak's camouflage patterns = partners for success. "Mossy Oak has exposed its brand globally through a licensing royalty model and an aggressive partner relationship. With approximately 1,000 licensed partners, Mossy Oak creates approximately 2 billion camouflage pattern impressions each year" (Forsyth, In Press, p. XX).

Plaid and the Tartan Trend. Like they have with camouflage, sport organizations, particularly universities, have embraced tartans as a new trend. In the spring of 2013, Oregon State University developed a tartan print as part of its athletic department rebranding (Rumpakis, Bee & Lee, Under Review). The OSU Beavers unveiled a new brand identity that included a unique tartan plaid: "the notches in the thick lines reference how beavers use their sharp front teeth to take down trees" (*Oregon State Media Guide*, p. 40). The white lines inside the tartan are comprised of both the "Oregon State" and "Beavers" wordmarks, making the tartan print even more exclusive and unique. The tartan is used sparingly, but it is distinctive and inimitable, something OSU was originally striving for with the implementation of the tartan as part of the rebrand.

Another example of universities using a tartan for branding purposes occurred in 2014 when the University of South Carolina Gamecocks commissioned a new collegiate tartan known as "Old Cocky" (Benette, 2014). In addition to the aforementioned tartans, Collegiate Tartan Apparel provides custom tartan prints for assorted universities. Founded in 2009, Collegiate Tartan Apparel "addresses the desire by students and alumni for high-quality apparel and accessories that express their school affiliation with style and sophistication" (About Us, 2016).

According to the company website:

> Collegiate Tartan Apparel works closely with its university clients to design the school's official 'tartan,' which is a design consisting of several colors of bands crisscrossed both horizontally and vertically. It might also be called a plaid, but the design is so specific in its colors and pattern that it is registered with the International Tartan Registry in Edinburgh, Scotland. (About Us, 2016)

Many schools have worked with Collegiate Tartan to develop an exclusive design, including Georgetown University, University of Kentucky, Marshall University and Purdue University, as well as a host of others (About Us, 2016).

The Radford Highlanders. Radford University in Virginia is home to the Highlanders. In the fall of 2016, the university introduced a new "branding system" aimed at setting the "brand direction of the department for the future" (Radford Athletics, 2016). This unveiling was the culmination of a process involving various institutional stakeholders, including administrators, alumni, coaches, current and former student-athletes, and community members.

Radford's new brand identity included new logos (primary and secondary marks), wordmarks, custom typography, uniforms, a new mascot, and a new online team shop. The athletic rebrand sought to provide a distinct and dynamic brand identity that paid homage to the university's history in the Virginia Highlands. Part of this homage was the incorporation of plaid into the school's logos and other brand identity elements and touchpoints.

Conclusion

This chapter addressed the use of color as an integral element of a sport organization's brand identity. Teams from the local and high school level right on through those in the professional ranks use one or more colors to identify themselves. Many use a signature color, one that can uniquely identify the organization from among a sea of competitors. Other organizations opt for a color palette that includes two or more colors used on a variety of touch-points across media. In addition, this chapter discussed the trend toward patterns (camouflage and tartan) as part of a sport organization's brand identity.

Chapter 4

Architecture, Interior Design, and Landscaping

If an organization wants to truly project its brand identity in every facet of its presentation, it has the ability to use its architecture and interior design as elements of its identity. This is one way to ensure that the identity is diffused not just through written, digital or televised communications, but also in person to fans and other stakeholders. The use of architecture and interior design to support brand identity promotion is paramount in the sport industry because tens of thousands of fans sit in the respective stadium or arena on a regular basis, and the media is broadcasting to innumerable people elsewhere.

The organization's environmental characteristics, such as its strategic use of color, texture, light, and information can aid in managing perceptions associated with the institutional environment (Wheeler, 2006). This can include connections to geographic considerations, as well as environmental factors such as cleanliness, durability, and sustainability (Hussain & Ferdous, 2015).

The sport industry internationally is rife with examples of creative stadiums and arenas, such as Boise State University's blue football turf (sometimes called "Smurf Turf" or "The Blue"), the tree-inspired basketball court at the University of Oregon, or the

National Aquatics Center in Beijing, China, built for the 2008 summer Olympics and known as "The Water Cube." Other stadiums stand out for their architectural genius. AT&T Stadium in Arlington, Texas, home of the Dallas Cowboys, is large: the fourth largest in the NFL, but its claim to architectural fame is that it's column-free, and the largest column-free "room" in the world. From a brand identity perspective, however, the most interesting stadium in the world might be Allianz Arena in Munich, Germany, home of two local soccer clubs. It was the first stadium in the world designed to change color depending on the color of the team playing inside (Allianz Arena, 2017).

Landscaping in a sport setting or on a university campus is perhaps the most ephemeral of brand identity elements, but it can also be used to great advantage if done strategically or for a long period of time. Ivy has been associated with elite colleges since the 1800s. The universities that now comprise the Ivy League have ivy climbing the walls of many buildings because the schools once had ivy planting ceremonies as part of class day activities.

Having a unique location enables sport organizations to attract the attention of in-person spectators who have the opportunity to physically experience the elements of the brand identity, but it also provides the exponentially larger television viewing audience the opportunity to experience it. If the venue, be it a stadium, arena or park, is creatively designed, the media covering the event might also provide additional opportunities for brand identity promotion. In college football, Bronco Stadium at Boise State University has what is colloquially known as the "Smurf Turf," the football team's artificial blue turf. The original blue turf was installed in 1986, and it has received a lot of attention from the local media, but gradually the attention tapered off. When the team moved into the more prestigious Mountain West Conference and began earning top rankings and bowl wins, the blue turf became a national story. The notoriety is evidenced by the fact that every day, at least a few tourists arrive on campus to ask permission to have their pictures taken on the turf. In addition to Boise State's Smurf Turf, other universities have also gotten into the colored turf game, including Eastern Washington University, which has a red field, and Coastal Carolina University, which has a teal field.

Sometimes a stadium or arena is not remarkable in its overall appearance, but it may have one unique feature that makes it a standout. For example, Fenway Park, home of the Boston Red Sox, has the "Green Monster," a 37-foot green wall in left field that also seats 269 people (Newcomb, 2014). Heinz Field, home of the NFL's Pittsburgh Steelers, has a digital scoreboard with a Heinz ketchup bottle on either side. When the team scores a touchdown, the ketchup bottles tilt to the side and the Jumbotron screens fills with red. The Durham Bulls, the AAA affiliate of the MLB's Tampa Bay Rays, has a sign known as the "Snorting Bull." Whenever a member of the home team scores a home run, several things happen as the player runs the bases: smoke puffs from the bull's nostrils, the bull's eyes light up red, and the tail wags. These three things also follow every Durham Bulls victory at the park. If a player hits the sign, which would be a home run, he wins a steak.

The Sporting Environment/Sportscape. Further points of connection can include the physical setting in which the sporting activities take place (Meir & Scott, 2007). Wakefield's notion of sportscape refers to:

> The entire built and managed environment that the fan sees when attending a sporting event. Managing the place is particularly important in sportscapes because fans spend hours in the place. In fact, the more time fans spend in the place, the more important the facility is in determining fan attendance. (Wakefield, 2016)

Sportscape factors include various factors that:

> influence how (dis)pleasurable fans feel the place is. These feelings influence fans' willingness to stay in the facility, spend money while in the facility, and to return in the future. While our focus is on the built environment, these same elements can be adapted for more flexible, open venues such as golf tournaments and other events. (Wakefield, 2016)

An example that illustrates the discomfort fans might feel watching an event, that might then turn them off to attending the team's future events, is the Carrier Dome at Syracuse University. It was named in 1979 in one of the first examples of a university selling naming rights. The Carrier Corporation, an air conditioning giant, made a $2.75 million gift, but because the Syracuse winters are notoriously cold and long, the decision was made to forgo air conditioning (Carlson, 2016a; 2016b).

The place of sport or the sport setting also has a variety of touch points, which can provide greater connectivity to support participants and other stakeholders associated with sport endeavors. Wakefield's sportscape factors include:

- *Aesthetics* (including architectural design, colors, and brand attractiveness)
- *Layout accessibility* (Convenience of getting in, moving around and exiting sportscape)
- *Seating comfort* (Spaciousness around seats and actual comfort of seat)
- *Electronic equipment and displays* (Includes scoreboards, video screens, and signage)
- *Cleanliness* (Condition of the seating area and other customer touchpoints, including restrooms, food service areas, and concourses) (Fetchko, Roy & Clow, 2013).

What Is the Local Fare?
Dodger Dogs and Memphis BBQ

In an effort to maximize food and beverage sales, many venues find it advantageous to brand certain offerings with popular locally or nationally recognized products (Mahoney, Esckilsen, Jeralds & Camp, 2015). Some sport organizations and venues have staple, and perhaps even iconic, food offerings. Consider the popularity and folklore associated with the iconic Dodger Dog.

Accordingly, organizations are able to benefit by selling foods that have a connection to geographic locations and cultural norms.

For example, fans attending sporting events in Chicago might seek a Chicago-style hot dog or deep dish pizza; likewise, individuals attending events in Philadelphia may desire a cheesesteak. Sporting events in Albuquerque are likely to provide items that have the local fare of green chilies. And of course, it would be natural that one could order some BBQ in locales such as Texas, Kansas City, and Memphis.

Wakefield (2016) recommends that sport teams and venues consider developing a "signature food item." Having a signature item that fans actually seek out, one that is even preferential to food options outside of the park, can be quite a coup. Wakefield presents notable examples, including BBQ in the form Rendezvous Nachos (AutoZone Park, Memphis, TN), pierogis (Jacobs Field, Cleveland, OH), and clam chowder (Fenway Park, Boston, MA).

There's Pride in Every Whataburger. Whataburger is distinctly Texas, while at the same time being distinctly Southern. The quick-service restaurant is a staple of the food culture in the Lone Star State while having a presence throughout the Deep South, particularly in the Gulf Coast states of Louisiana, Mississippi, Alabama, and Florida. The food chain is noted for its distinctive organizational brand identity, including its unique, self-descriptive name (note: the animated series *King of the Hill* even paid homage by referencing the Texas chain "Want-A-Burger" during its run), its iconic W logo, orange and white color scheme, its common use of A-frame restaurants, and taglines such as "There's pride in every Whataburger."

While there are Whataburger franchises located in 10 states in the US, its core is the state of Texas, where there are more than 650 restaurants; there are just fewer than 150 restaurants in the other nine states combined (https://locations.whataburger.com/index.html). As part of Whataburger's connection to the south, but most particularly Texas, the company has engaged in many school and university-based initiatives. These include both sport and non-sport activities (e.g., elementary schools having a What a Night or high schools having a Whataburger Bash).

In terms of connection to sport, the company has served as title sponsor of events (e.g., Whataburger College Classic) and even had stadium naming rights (minor league baseball's Whataburger Field in Corpus Christi, TX). Additionally, Whataburger is a sponsor of athletic programs at universities throughout the State of Texas, including Texas A&M University, Sam Houston State University, Rice University, and the University of Texas at San Antonio. The company has also had an extended connection to sport via its clever use of social media. For example, the @Whataburger account tweets various messages conveying the love of their food, customers, Texas, the South, and sport to its 800,000+ followers. Social media and popular press have allowed the legend of Whataburger to grow, fueling the love of their devoted patrons and adding to the myth for those not fortunate enough to live within driving distance of a restaurant.

Branding through Innovation. On October 29, 2016, the University of Wyoming broke ground on the Mick and Susie McMurry High Altitude Performance Center (HAPC). This venue will serve as one of the preeminent athletic facilities in the country by featuring 71,000 square feet of new space as it expands the already existing Curtis and Marian Rochelle Athletics Center to over 118,000 square feet ("Mick and Susie McMurry High Altitude Performance Center Groundbreaking Held Saturday," 2016).

University of Wyoming's head football coach Craig Bohl stated that "The Mick and Susie McMurry High Altitude Performance Center will redefine Cowboy football" as it will "play a critical role in our vision of recruiting to what we call the Wyoming Profile. That recruiting effort involves attracting a young man who is committed to earning a meaningful degree from an outstanding academic institution and has a laser-like focus to win Mountain West Conference championships. The High Altitude Performance Center will put us at the top of the league in terms of training and academic facilities, which is where we also aspire to be on the field of competition" ("Mick and Susie McMurry High Altitude Performance Center Groundbreaking Held Saturday," 2016).

The implementation of the building initiative at the University of Wyoming is a prime example of institutional goals sought by schools as they seek to engage in the so-called intercollegiate "arms race." Eitzen (2016) elaborates on the "athletic arms race" as a strategy where institutions devote increasing revenue and expenditures to keep up with or surpass the athletic competition.

> To make money, an athletic department must spend money on increasing the recruiting budget, hiring more fundraisers and marketing personnel, improving practice facilities, adding new seating in the stadiums and arenas (especially skyboxes), purchasing the latest equipment, and building expensive new sports annexes with lavish locker rooms, weight rooms, training rooms, meeting rooms, lounges, and offices for the coaches and athletic administrators. In short, this "arms race" is an attempt to improve the school's overall image, impress alumni, and especially wow recruits. (Eitzen, 2016, p. 183)

Various other factors such as architecture, building materials, landscaping, and other venue factors can serve as strong visual identity components. Various implementations are used to serve as points of connection ranging from live habitats on campus housing beloved mascots to implementing iconic signifiers that serve as points of identification and inspiration for followers of brands. For example, Virginia Tech's use of Hokie Stone and Clemson's famed Tiger Paw hole provide valuable examples of such visual identifiers.

Hokie Stone. Virginia Tech uses the Collegiate Gothic style, but it is fortunate enough to mine its own limestone on the outskirts of Blacksburg, where its campus is located. The limestone is so closely associated with Virginia Tech that it is now called "Hokie Stone," after the school's name for its athletic teams—and its more ardent fans.

Clemson's Tiger Paw Hole. More modern uses of landscaping as a brand identity element have extended to include campus golf courses. The 17th hole at The Walker Course at Clemson University is the course's signature hole. In true Clemson Tiger spirit, the hole is landscaped as a tiger's paw. The green is the main pad of the tiger's paw, while the four remaining pads serve as bunkers or sand traps.

Bass Pro Shops: Selling Nature. Bass Pro Shops provides a valuable look into the connection between sport and nature. Bass Pro Shops sells products that inspire people to experience the great outdoors and hopefully pass on the love of nature to others. Bass Pro Shops spreads affinity for the outdoors in various ways, including through nature-themed destinations such as Outdoor World, Big Cedar Lodge, and Dogwood Canyon Ranch.

- *Outdoor World–Springfield, Missouri: The Granddaddy of All Outdoor Stores.* With more than 4 million people visiting annually, the Outdoor World store in Springfield, Missouri is recognized as Bass Pro Shops' "flagship store." Comprised of 300,000 plus square feet of retail space, complemented by elaborate architecture, a wildlife museum, eye-catching waterfalls, gigantic aquariums, and various restaurants, this outdoor store has become one of Missouri's premier tourist attractions.
- *Big Cedar Lodge.* Resting on the banks of Table Rock Lake near Branson, Missouri, Big Cedar Lodge is an 850-acre resort where guests can experience America's sporting traditions and outdoor activities.
- *Dogwood Canyon Nature Park.* Dogwood Canyon Nature Park is a 10,000-acre wilderness heaven that is situated in the Missouri Ozarks, which has been certified as an Audubon International Signature Sanctuary. This getaway is open to the public for animal watchers, tram tours, hiking, biking, horseback riding, fishing and more (Forsyth & Lee, In Press).

Conclusion

This chapter has explored the use of architecture and interior design, as well as landscaping, in a sport organization's brand identity. College and professional sport programs have long recognized the importance of having attractive and comfortable buildings and arenas to house their teams and events, but there is an increased focus on the more tangential elements, such as concession offerings and concourse activities. The concept even stretches as far as the habitats for live animal mascots that represent the university. In addition to the previously discussed elements of name, logo, tagline and colors, architecture and landscaping provide a dynamic way to promote any sport organization's brand identity.

Chapter 5

Uniforms, Clothing and Game Day Rituals

One of the ways in which an organization can personify its brand identity is through the appearance of its employees. In sport, uniforms can include athletic uniforms as well as work uniforms (team management, stadium staff, concession staff and custodial staff). Beyond the notion of uniforms, various other organizational clothing considerations help project an organization's brand identity. This can include traditional attire worn by organizational representatives (e.g., college professors wearing "dress clothes" and coaches wearing traditional coaching attire), and in some cases, the sport organization's fans become willing participants in the organization's projection of its brand identity.

Employee Uniforms. Workplace uniforms serve a variety of purposes. Initially, they serve as a brand recognition point for consumers and guests. They also provide consistency, "uniformity," which keeps inappropriate attire out of the organization. Inappropriate attire could come in the form of something that is not representative of the quality, look and content the organization seeks to project. Beyond such controls, workplace attire can be helpful as a branding touchpoint: consider the white short-sleeve dress shirts and solid black ties worn by members of Best Buy's "Geek Squad," or the referee-inspired uniform of Foot Locker employees.

Athletic Uniforms. Uniforms have become not only a highly visible element of organizational brand identity but also a key weapon that sport organizations have used to keep up with the athletic "arms race." While the typical examples of sport-related "arms race" weapons pertain to athletic venues and other luxury resources, uniforms have proven to be a major and distinguishable artifact that can serve as valuable calling cards for sport organizations.

There are athletic programs that have been noted for their innovative use of uniforms, including presentation formats and variations available. This is even been a point of controversy with regard to athlete recruitment of young and impressionable teenagers, since they may be persuaded by schools with the superficial: flashy designs and captivating uniform styles.

The appreciation and study of uniforms have reached the point where various websites and social media accounts examine nuances, attributes, and variations associated with the sport uniform. Perhaps the best known of these is the ESPN-affiliated *Uni Watch* site, which professes to be "Obsessed with the aesthetics of athletics" (www.uni-watch.com).

Various uniform color considerations and combinations were addressed in Chapter 3. In addition to simple color, there are various iconic uniforms in the landscape of sport. Consider the iconic pinstripes of the New York Yankees, the legendary stars and stripes on the uniforms of the Harlem Globetrotters, or the standout uniforms of teams such as the Los Angeles Lakers, Chicago Cubs, and the Dallas Cowboys. Beyond these time-tested uniforms, various unique uniforms have enjoyed longevity in the annals of sport folklore: the infamous MLB's Houston Astros' "Tequila Sunrise" jerseys of the 1970s and 80s, and the iconic MLB Pittsburgh Pirates pillbox hats of the 1970s are popular with sport fans, uniform enthusiasts, and collectors alike. Uniforms such as these have continued to live on in various throwback iterations and other thematic homages.

Even in a world replete with uniforms of all styles and colors, some institutions seem to stand out from the crowd. Perhaps no other college program is more noted for its prolific uniforms than the University of Oregon Ducks football team. The Ducks are the showcase school for the Nike uniform and apparel empire. The school's proximity to Nike headquarters in Beaverton, Oregon, and its status as the company founder Phil Knight's alma mater, has made the school a showpiece in the Nike program that provides uniforms to university athletic teams. The Oregon Ducks have become somewhat famous for their seemingly unlimited assortment of uniform combinations.

The University of Maryland, dubbed the "Oregon of the East," is Under Armour's counterpart for the Nike juggernaut. The Maryland Terrapins complement their unique nickname with an assortment of standout uniform options. Under Armour's founder, Kevin Plank, is a former Maryland football player and as his company has flourished, so has the University of Maryland's athletic brand identity offerings.

Beyond Oregon and Maryland, other schools such as Baylor University and Oklahoma State have emerged as innovative uniform implementers. Schools such as these and legions of others use their partnership with outfitters such as Nike and its Jordan Brand, Under Armour, and adidas to regularly try and one-up the competition.

Customary Attire. As was addressed previously, customary attire in an organization comprises a de facto uniform in a variety of sport-related settings. In university settings, various university employees wear attire appropriate for the jobs and the overall work environment. For example, administrators and professors typically wear dress clothes and business casual attire. College athletic department employees may wear similar attire depending on the occasion, however, the typical athletic department attire may generally consist predominantly of licensed university athletic gear. Coaches typically wear such attire in office environments, but different attire during game-time situations. Sports such as basketball often adopt a more professional style of dress, such as business attire (e.g., suits, coat, and ties). Baseball head coaches follow the customary practice of wearing their team's uniform. Football has developed a clothing culture unto itself. For example, certain coaches opt for polo shirts while others opt for pullovers. In the NFL, Bill Belichick has made a fashion statement—or principle—of his own:

> According to sources through the years, after Reebok inked a reported $250 million deal as the official outfitter of the NFL in the early 2000s, one of the tenets of the contract was that coaches would wear their gear. Belichick rejected the concept on principle, arguing that some NFL executive in New York shouldn't be telling grown men how to dress ... That didn't mean he could ignore it forever, so when presented with all of the acceptable items to wear, Belichick purposefully chose what he believed was the least fashionable choice ... the humble grey hoodie. He soon even chopped the sleeves off of it, often with crooked and sloppy cuts, perhaps in an effort to make it less attractive. (Chase, 2015)

"When in Rome" (Dressing for the Occasion). Sporting events provide regular opportunities for fans to show their allegiance to their teams. Fans attending games regularly opt to wear licensed merchandise from their favorite team, or at least the team's colors on shirts, hats, uniforms, etc. In school settings, wearing school colors and items emblazoned with school names and logos allows individuals to represent their school proudly. For a sampling of licensed branded merchandise, consider the plethora of items that are available in school brick and mortar bookstores or through online sites such as Fanatics.

Having the Look. When people go the Masters or the Players Championship, they may dress differently than usual. They may look like they are about to play a round, even though they are just there as spectators. Fans may even wear purposely outlandish clothing that would make Ian Poulter or the late Payne Stewart proud. This could include wearing Loudmouth Golf pants or shorts. Bloomberg Business identified Loudmouth's gear as being "The Most Outrageous Golf Clothes You Can Buy" ("The Most Outrageous Golf Clothes You Can Buy," 2014).

Cosplay? The world of cosplay is visible on shows such as *SyFy's Heroes of Cosplay* and many episodes of the hit sitcom *The Big Bang Theory*. While cosplay, or dressing up as fictional characters such as superheroes or cartoon characters, is something generally reserved for individuals attending events akin to Comic Con, sport spectators routinely take part in the dress-up festivities. Other than perhaps Halloween or the occasional costume party, the average person does not get many opportunities to don costumes. Sport venues have become environments where the practice of donning random costumes is both commonplace and accepted. Consider an LSU fan who is fully decked out in a Purple and Gold superhero costume or a Minnesota fan dressed as a popular Pokémon character as part of game-day festivities.

Ceremonial Garb. Universities are perhaps the institutions most entrenched in traditional and ceremonial garb. The custom of wearing academic regalia dates back to the 12th and 13th centuries when universities were just being set up and academics wore them to stay warm in cold buildings. Today, attendees at commencement ceremonies around the world can easily identify the pedigree of the university's professors by looking at the length, style, and color of the hood and gown the professor is wearing (Historical Overview of the Academic Costume Code, 2017).

In a sport context, ceremonial attire is traditional in a variety of settings: the Olympic Games and in career celebratory ceremonies, such as wearing the ceremonial gold jacket during enshrinement to the Pro Football Hall of Fame, or the presentation of the famed green jacket at the PGA Tour's Masters at Augusta and the yellow jersey of the Tour de France.

Uniform Debates: The Collegiate Beach Volleyball "Dress Code"

Branding the sport of collegiate beach volleyball requires a discussion on the uniforms. The culture of professional volleyball, both beach and indoor, includes sponsorship advertising on the uniforms. Use of this "signage space" is restricted by NCAA rules in collegiate sand volleyball: there may be one sport brand logo on each piece of clothing, not to exceed 2½ inches. This is always the manufacturer of the garment and not a direct advertisement.

The uniform of professional beach volleyball, which is overseen by the Federation Internationale de Volleyball (FIVB), is a two-piece uniform that can be worn comfortably in the heat. The uniform rules of the FIVB and the NCAA determine minimum uniform coverage based on the expectations of being able to see the player's numbers and school or country names. It should be noted that when it is cold, the athletes wear uniforms that are more appropriate for the weather. Somewhat controversial is the NCAA restriction of the collegiate beach volleyball uniform. It must cover the midsection while standing (meaning much like an indoor jersey, it can move up during intense movement). There are two sides to the uniform debate. The NCAA requires the uniform to cover the midsection to downplay the sexist nature of the sport culture. The uniform covering the midsection would separate it and the competition of the athletes from simply "girls in bikinis." However, the sport on a professional level, globally, is played in a two-piece uniform. The traditional two-piece or bikini uniform is what people expect to see, and there may be a specific segment of the target market that would be interested in seeing the sport played in the two-piece uniforms. Understandably, the NCAA is trying to protect its female athletes from sexist and negative media attention.

Cowboy Tough. Wyoming coach Craig Bohl stresses being "cowboy tough" (#CowboyTough). When he came to the University of Wyoming, he got rid of all of the "fancy uniforms" and said that his team would have only two uniforms—a home uniform and an away uniform. Wyoming is a minimalist team: it simply uses its brown and yellow/gold color palette with its iconic cowboy logo and "Old West" font (From *CBS Sports Network* broadcast of Wyoming's upset of Boise State, October 29, 2016).

Get Your Kicks. Shoes can be great identifiers for various sport organizations and individuals. Consider the various standout sneaker lines that have impacted fashion, both within sport settings and without. Whether it is sneakerheads sporting their extensive collection, an athlete wearing the latest adidas Yeezy cleats, or assorted individuals showing off their Jordans, Lebrons, or Steph Curry's. In today's world, coaches such as Mississippi State University football coach Dan Mullen can earn "street cred" with his athletes and potential recruits by wearing the latest shoes that resonate with those athletes and fans alike.

Sport Traditions

University traditions can provide important threads in the fabric of sport organizations. "Tradition-rich" schools, such as Texas A&M, the University Alabama, and the University of Tennessee are all noted for their extensive array of traditions. Consider some other gameday sport traditions: the Clemson University football team runs down "The Hill" toward Howard's Rock, which each player touches for luck before every home game; Ohio State University's band performs the Script Ohio formation at football games, with a chosen person "dotting the I"; other, less official traditions include burning couches at West Virginia University, "sailgating" at the University of Washington, or even the incessant yelling by the "Cameron Crazies" at Duke University home basketball games.

Further examples of tradition are evident on ESPN's *College GameDay* broadcasts. Notable moments include host Lee Corso's headgear selection, the arrival of weekly guest pickers, the masses of fans with creative signs, and even the weekly appearance of Washington State University's flag (Ol' Crimson), which has made weekly appearances on the show for years.

Higher education institutions, while steeped in sports tradition, certainly do not corner the market on them. Consider some of the notable professional sport traditions, such as throwing an octopus after a goal at Detroit Red Wings games, a tradition that dates back to the 1950s; throwing back home runs by opposing teams at Chicago Cubs games, or the assorted antics of the Portland Timbers' Timber Army.

Sport Rivalries

Rivalries can provide significant opportunities to promote the brand identity of sport organizations, as these rivalries reflect the significant role of how supporters identify with their beloved teams

(Smith & Schwartz, 2003). Accordingly, sport properties are able to promote rivalry for associated institutional benefits (Lee, Zapalac & Godfrey, Under Review). Unsurprisingly, rivalry games can serve as appointment viewing, either in person or through media consumption.

Professional sport is noted for storied rivalries. Consider the rivalry in Major League Baseball between the New York Yankees and the Boston Red Sox, the Dallas Cowboys and the Washington Redskins, the Portland Timbers and the Washington Sounders, or any number of other storied rivalries impacting professional sport in the United States or in sport around the globe.

Rivalries comprise a major part of the world of collegiate sport. Such collegiate rivalries have official names, colloquial nicknames, and even branded corporate names (Hutchinson, Havard, Berg & Ryan, 2016). For example, consider noted rivalries such as Alabama and Auburn's annual football showdown known as the Iron Bowl, the rivalry between the University of Oklahoma and Oklahoma State University, which is known as the "Bedlam Series"—or as it is now known officially as "The Blue Cross and Blue Shield of Oklahoma Bedlam Series" ("Blue Cross Blue Shield of Oklahoma named title sponsor for Bedlam Series," 2016).

Colloquially named rivalries have also become a part of our sport vernacular. A classic example of this is the longtime football rivalry between the University of Georgia and the University of Florida. This annual game has been called the "World's Largest Outdoor Cocktail Party," although that name has not been officially embraced by either university, and both schools have publicly distanced themselves from any such association.

The storied rivalry between the University of Oklahoma Sooners and the University of Texas Longhorns provides an interesting example of sport rivalry nomenclature. This intense rivalry was previously known as the "Red River Shootout," and this name was later changed to the "the Red River Rivalry"—and ultimately "the Red River Classic." This change demonstrates a shift in naming practices, including a politically correct movement away from gun connotations.

Conclusion

This chapter has discussed the idea of a sport organization's apparel and uniforms as an integral element of the organization's brand identity. Organizations like the University of Oregon Ducks football team have made their names because of the variety of uniforms they wear. Others, like Bill Belichick of the New England Patriots, have become famous for what he *will not* wear on the field. Another way that organizations reflect their identities is through the many traditions and activities embraced and undertaken in their sport on behalf of the organization. Many of these official traditions are steeped in an organization or sport programs' history, but ardent fans help build the actions into traditions.

Chapter 6

Actions and Behaviors

Beyond communicating the brand identity of a sport organization, the collective and individual actions of organizational participants, employees, and other stakeholders are significant. These behaviors can provide both a positive and negative influence, so organizations are to be mindful of the ramifications of personal actions (or lack thereof) and behaviors.

For example, if a sport organization is engaged in community initiatives where individuals are wearing organizational gear and they are being featured on a local media outlet sharing the latest positive outcomes, the organization's brand identity can be positively impacted. Alternatively, an initiative associated with practices that bring about negative connotations can be detrimental to the reputation of not only the organization or team but representatives and partnering businesses (i.e., sponsors). Moreover, the spillover effect of both positive and negative associations may be attributed to organizational representatives, particularly those serving as "faces" of the programs. Accordingly, it is of great importance to enact appropriate safeguards, including educating participants that they serve as de facto "ambassadors" of the organizations and their program offerings. Additionally, organization-related actions and behaviors have an impact on the program—whether positively or negatively. Upcoming passages provide samples of actions, behaviors, and notable people impacting sport-related brand identities.

Sport and Celebrity

Sport is filled with many celebrities and moments that are made for developing opportunities for fame. In the context of sport, some serve the role of "reluctant celebrity," while others seemingly live for the spotlight. Athletes that have historically been willing to go to great ends to further their fame include the NBA's Dennis Rodman and the NFL's Brian Bosworth, Terrell Owens, and Deion Sanders. Others, like the NBA's Michael Jordan and the MLB's Derek Jeter, have been noted for their accomplishment while remaining more private and understated about their public personas (Lee & Laucella, 2011).

An interesting consideration of the concept of celebrity is the notion of niche celebrities. By nature, some "celebrities" are famous only in small, niche markets. This can be the case for circles ranging from gospel singers to modern artists to certain political pundits. In some circles, those in the know would identify certain individuals as celebrities, but those unfamiliar with that scene may have no awareness of that person or their "fame" (Lee & Laucella, 2011).

In sport, there are various examples. For example, Professional Bull Riders (PBR) star Ryan Dirteater, dominant professional bowler Jason Belmonte, or preeminent professional skateboarder Theotis Beasley have amassed fame that really only exists in the circle of devoted rodeo, bowling or skateboarding fans, respectively.

Celebrity and Endorsements. Successfully tying mass emotional appeal to sport celebrities provides tremendous opportunities for brand affinity. The concepts of celebrity and brand personality complement each other, as the notions of the trustworthiness of celebrity endorsers can transmit awareness and acceptability for brands (Lee & Miloch, 2011). As such, the cultivation and promotion of personal brands provide identifiability and differentiation through reputation, appearance, affinity, and other characteristics (Lee & Laucella, 2011).

As athletes garner significant media coverage, particularly in the geographic areas where they reside and compete, a solid foundation is built for appeal and resonance with desired audiences. Noted athletes (and former athletes) such as the NFL's Brett Favre and Tom Brady, NASCAR's Dale Earnhardt Jr., the NBA's LeBron James, and the NFL's Peyton Manning have been positioned as celebrities whose fame has raised their profile far beyond their athletic accomplishments. Such individuals are examples of those sport personalities that are able to parlay their visibility and appeal into relationships with corporate partners seeking benefits associated with the celebrity's star power.

Effective cultivation of an individual's brand can generate great awareness and even loyalty among consumers (Lee & Miloch, 2011). Brand loyalty is key in an organization's marketing efforts: perception and positioning aid in seeking to build and enhance relationships with consumers who are brand-loyal, which can translate into other favorable behaviors (Lee & Miloch, 2011). For example, brand loyalty can be seen in consumer behaviors such as buying endorsed products (e.g., surfer Kelly Slater and Quiksilver products) or by certain individuals in association with products associated with organizations (e.g., the association of Jimmie Johnson with Lowe's).

The association of celebrity and the presence of notable personal brands extends beyond just "star" athletes. Besides athletes, notable individual personal brands include coaches, administrators or management and ownership, and more. Such individuals are able to serve as "faces" of the organization. Consider the following examples:

- Owner: Jerry Jones, Mark Cuban, George Steinbrenner, Bubba Watson (Minor League Owner)
- Executive: Billy Bean, Theo Epstein, Phil Jackson, John Elway
- School Administrator: Gordon Gee, Jim Tressel, Jeff Long
- Coach: Nick Saban, Dabo Sweeney, Joe Madden
- Player: Tom Brady, LeBron James, Serena Williams
- Supporter/Donor: T. Boone Pickens, Phil Knight, Kevin Plank
- Fan: Spike Lee, Jack Nicholson, Larry the Cable Guy
- Fan groups: Dawg Pound, Cameron Crazies, FSU Animals
- Actions/Behaviors: The UNF "Band Kid"; Garnet and Gold Guys at Florida State; Fireman Ed (Jets); Hoggettes (Redskins)

- Alumni: Shaquille O'Neal, Matthew McConaughey, Ashley Judd

In addition to the aforementioned examples, more detailed profiles will be provided throughout the remainder of this chapter. Further, Table 4 provides further examples of personal branding and brand identity by detailing sample "branded features" associated with sport personalities. There is a column where individuals can consider their own notable examples as a food-for-thought exercise.

Would You Rather Be John Daly or Boo Weekley? Individuals such as John Daly and Boo Weekley have left indelible marks on the sport of golf. These two individuals stand out in the "gentleman's game" like few others. Early in his career, John Daly was noted for his "good ole' boy" persona, his country roots, his blonde mullet, and his tendency to overindulge. He was also noted for his ability to drive a golf ball, his willingness to buck the system, and his legions of devoted followers. As time went by, Daly remained in the public eye, but in recent years he has garnered more attention for his unique fashion sense than his playing successes. As one of the preeminent ambassadors of the Loudmouth Golf brand, Daly has been noticed wearing a wide assortment of eye-catching golfwear. His gear of choice includes outlandish patterns such as paisleys, plaids, stripes, argyle, flags, and much more.

Boo Weekley has also tapped into the "good ole' boy" vibe, although he is more likely to represent "camouflage culture" than vibrantly loud pants. By partnering with companies such as Realtree, Weekley dons camouflage and orange attire that evokes notions of the great outdoors and hunting.

Case in Point: The WWE's A. J. Styles. Professional wrestling is part performance art and part morality play, with a sizable mix of athleticism and pageantry. The WWE is the predominant organization in the professional wrestling industry and promotes its product as a distinct brand of "sports entertainment." Through the years, the WWE has produced various "superstars" (WWE terminology for wrestlers). This includes crossover stars such as Hulk Hogan, "Stone Cold" Steve Austin, Dwayne Johnson (aka The Rock), and John

Table 4: Sample Branded Features— Examples and Considerations

Sample Branded "Features"	Provided Example(s)	Provide Your Own Example
"Hair Ball"? Branded Hairdos	David Beckham. His various hairstyles through the years have been trendsetters.	1. 2. 3.
Branded Beards	James Harden	1. 2. 3.
Branded Mustaches	Rollie Fingers (Hall of Fame baseball player) & Shad Khan (Jacksonville Jaguars owner)	1. 2. 3.
Branded Tattoos	Combat sports fighters such as Conor McGregor and Mike Tyson, as well as professional wrestlers such as Bill Goldberg and Dwayne "The Rock" Johnson, are noted for their identifiable tattoos	1. 2. 3.
Fashionistas	Athletes such as David Beckham, Cristiano Ronaldo, and Maria Sharapova are noted fashion icons. Furthermore, Serena Williams has had iconic fashion moments occurring on the tennis court.	1. 2. 3.

Cena. In addition to these more mainstream pop culture icons, the WWE has also featured a number of wrestling stars that demonstrate various identity elements. A prime example of this is A.J. Styles. Styles, whose real name is Alan Jones (hence the wrestling name "A.J."), is a visible face of the "pseudo-sport" of professional wrestling. He is one of the most famous wrestlers in the world because he has built a reputation as a stellar performer in small independent promotions as well as with large companies around the world. Upon entering the WWE, Styles instantly became a sensation that resonated with the fans. Aside from his gimmicked professional wrestling name, he has long held the nickname "The "Phenomenal One." As his character evolved from a "face" good guy to a "heel" bad guy figure, he kept that nickname, but also used others—"The Face that Runs the Place" and "The Champ that Runs the Camp"—to raise the ire of the crowd (and further endear himself to his legions of fans).

Styles' personal appearance and names and nicknames are just the tips of the brand identity iceberg. He employs a high flying and explosive offensive style that features his "signature moves": the "Styles Clash" and the "Phenomenal Forearm." His attire (in essence his uniform) also conveys a distinct brand identity. Aside from customary tights adorned with his P1 logo (for Phenomenal One), boots, and knee and elbow pads, Styles also wears branded gloves (which can, of course, be purchased by kids and adults alike at the WWE online shop).

On his way to the ring, Styles might also be seen wearing additional items, such as sleeveless t-shirts, a leather vest with Japanese writing (signifying his time and success in Japan), and when in possession of one, a championship belt. Styles' clothing only helps to accentuate his look as he enters the ring with his signature swagger, complete with customary hand gestures and poses. All of this transpires as he is accompanied by one of the WWE's more recognizable sonic branding efforts: his theme song, "Phenomenal," which is a powerful, Southern hip-hop-inspired song replete with catchy hooks; the song can also be purchased on iTunes.

Individuality and Self-Promotion in Track and Field. Track and field are sports that feature displays of individuality while providing unique opportunities for self-promotion. Such displays of self-promotion are practical attempts to attract publicity and open pathways for recognition, leading to prospects for sponsorship and endorsements (Lee, Conrad & Thomas, 2013) or to aid in the process of "branding" through vividly displayed athletic performance, coupled with individuality and fashion sense (Lee, Conrad & Thomas, 2013).

The landscape of American track and field has seen the emergence and admiration of some of the most storied sport heroes in the history of the country. A notable example of track and field celebrity and sport-powered branding was seen in the late Olympic hero Florence Griffith-Joyner. "Flo-Jo" was celebrated for her innovative fashion sense, stunning looks, exceptionally long nails, and trademark track uniforms (Lee, Conrad & Thomas, 2013). Since Flo-Jo, aspiring track and field stars have regularly sought to establish such an image and Flo-Jo's level of adulation.

Pioneers of Fitness. The infamous Charles Atlas and Jack LaLanne were early pioneers and have become icons in the bodybuilding movement. Charles Atlas' system of "Dynamic Tension" and the associated symbolic advertisements have left indelible marks on the physical fitness industry. Advertisements associated with Atlas' training system were executed in many forms, but were generally centered on a puny person becoming more muscular (such as "The Insult that Made a Man out of Mac" advertisement) (About Charles Atlas, 2016).

Jack LaLanne, who was most often seen in his tight fitting blue jumpsuit, was another iconic figure in the world of health and fitness. Jack LaLanne opened the first health club in the United States in 1936 and introduced the first television show dedicated to exercise and fitness in 1951 entitled *The Jack LaLanne Show*. His passion for health and fitness motivated Americans to exercise and eat healthy. His television show was primarily targeted toward homemakers who were able to use items around the house to participate in his exercise routines. LaLanne died at the age of 97 and continued to promote fitness up until his death (Jack LaLanne Biography, 2014).

Music to My Ears

There are various musical and auditory elements that impact sport brand identity. For example, the presence of anthems is common in the sport landscape. The term *anthem* can identify musical works that serve a multitude of purposes. "In particular, the term *anthem* is used to describe musical works that serve a variety of purposes, including for religious ceremonies, as symbols of national pride and identity in the case of national anthems, and for other purposes such as school songs/fight songs" (Lee & Whisenant, 2011, p. 65).

Anthems are used in myriad sport settings, from Little League opening day ceremonies to high school athletics events to professional sporting events and even as part of international sporting events, such as the Olympic Games. In American sport folklore, marquee sporting events have hosted some memorable renditions of the U.S. national anthem. Namely, Marvin Gaye's acclaimed rendition of the national anthem at the 1983 NBA All-Star Game and Whitney Houston's 1991 Super Bowl national anthem performance at the tail end of Operation Desert Storm have gone down as iconic moments in American sport—and music—history (Lee & Whisenant, 2011).

Furthermore, sport anthems (or stadium anthems) also provide memorable examples of sport brand identity. While implementation of anthems abounds in sport settings on both large and small scales, classic examples of such "sport anthems" include "Sweet Home Alabama" at University of Alabama's Crimson Tide sporting events, "Sweet Caroline" during the "seventh inning stretch" at Boston Red Sox home games, or the infamous practice of playing "Jump Around" at University of Wisconsin football games.

Because the songs and the performances are important aspects of sport brand identity, the performers and participants are key players. For example, in interscholastic and collegiate sport settings, the bands themselves are symbols of a specific culture. University marching bands serve as "modern totems" that allow groups to differentiate themselves from others. Consider performances by the "Fightin' Texas Aggie Band" from Texas A&M, or the famed

"Marching Storm" band of Prairie View A&M University, which denotes the spirit of this Historically Black College and University (HBCU).

Even in band performances, specific band members are able to stand out as individual performers even in the midst of the larger group setting. For example, in 2015, the University of North Florida Ospreys men's basketball team made its maiden voyage into postseason play by earning its first bid to the NCAA Tournament. As this was the team's first trip to the "Big Dance," the team and the school were profiled by various news outlets, including an on-campus profile hosted by *ESPN* anchor and school alumnus and former Osprey athlete Sara Walsh. This feature highlighted UNF's beautiful campus, the team's high-energy head coach, and the notorious "UNF Band Kid." UNF's Band Kid became an instant media sensation when his halftime antics were profiled by the "Worldwide Sports Leader."

During home games, the UNF Band Kid has all eyes on him in anticipation of the one-man-show that transpires once the DJ Snake and Lil' Jon song "Turn Down for What" is cued up. Once the song comes on, the student, who is a prominent fixture in the school's pep band, gyrates and convulses with arms flailing wildly, and all of this culminates with a fellow band member dousing the exhausted performer with water. This individual's performance lives on in infamy through YouTube.

Texas Schools Love Their Hand Signs. An interesting and significant action that can reflect a brand identity in sport is the use of hand gestures. A number of prominent examples can be found in institutions of higher education in the state of Texas, ranging from the "Guns up" of Texas Tech to the "Hook 'em Horns" symbol of the University of Texas, to the "Gig 'em" of Texas A&M. Clearly, identifiable hand gestures connect fans and provide a sense of community and a source of communication, identification, and differentiation for followers of the schools (see Table 5).

Table 5: Sample Activity—Identify the Hand Gesture

Name of University	Name the Mascot	Identify the "Hand Gesture"	Symbolic Meaning
University of Texas			
Texas A&M			
TCU			
University of Houston			
SMU			
Texas Tech			
Sam Houston State			
Texas State			
Stephen F. Austin State University			
Rice			
Others???			

Negative Actions and Behaviors

The Super Bowl of Criminal Jocks. The nexus of sport and criminal behavior is manifest in many forms (Lee & Lee, 2009), including the common presence of "criminal jocks" (Sweeney & Lee, 2014). The visibility of criminal jocks has garnered great media attention and sparked debate among sport consumers. Both historically and more recently, the National Football League (NFL) has been prominently associated with criminal jocks. In the NFL, two teams in the league have tallied enough arrests in recent history to be en route to the "Super Bowl of Criminal Jocks" (Sweeney & Lee, 2014).

The Cincinnati Bengals are most prominent in terms of being on the wrong end of the criminal justice system, and they have been closely contested in recent years by the small-market franchise, the Minnesota Vikings. These two franchises have earned the distinction of being the "poster children" of the NFL's "criminal jocks." The Bengals have steadily built a reputation for undesirable characteristics, such as underperforming and players' running afoul of the law (Sweeney & Lee, 2011). Justifiably so, the Bengals garnered their reputation by employing players who have been arrested or charged with crimes during their employment (e.g., Nate Webster, Chris Henry, Odell Thurman), as well as serving as a new home to players who are no strangers to legal issues while on other NFL rosters (e.g., "Pacman" Jones, Tank Johnson, Cedric Benson). The Bengals franchise has cemented its reputation as housing "criminal jocks," particularly after making good on their promise to keep rookie linebacker Brandon Joiner, who was sentenced to three years in prison on two counts of aggravated robbery and one count of felony drug possession just weeks after his 2012 contract signing.

Fumbling in the Red Zone: The NFL and Domestic Violence. The NFL has taken various public relations hits pertaining to league representatives being embroiled in player-inflicted domestic violence crimes. While the NFL is not alone in confronting the problem of domestic violence, the League has been connected to many high-profile scandals. The negative backlash the NFL received was instrumental in spurring the league on to establish policies aimed at eliminating the issue of player-inflicted violence and domestic violence in the NFL.

NASCAR and the Confederate Flag. NASCAR's legion of devoted fans flock to race tracks across the country to witness the sporting spectacle, which is replete with incredible sights and thunderous sounds of powerful cars racing at speeds that often exceed 180 miles per hour (Lee, Bernthal, Whisenant & Mullane, 2010).

NASCAR is a sport born in the Southeastern United States that has traditionally garnered a reputation for being a Southern enterprise (Lee et al., 2008). Because the sport has had to contend with the stereotype of being a "redneck," "good ole' boy," Southern sport, there is a concern that these perceptions could hamper the racing series' ability to attract a new, more demographically diverse fan following as well as sponsors (Lee et al., 2008).

Particularly problematic for NASCAR has been the negative attention focused on the presence of Confederate flags at race venues. As time went by, NASCAR officials deliberated the public stance they wanted to take on the matter and have actually discouraged the flying of Confederate flags at race venues, going so far as to conduct flag swaps: American flags for individuals turning in their Confederate flags.

Baylor University and the Art of Paradox. Baylor University in Waco, Texas, is a university steeped in conservative tradition. While the university has various positive associations, the institution is not without its critics, scandals, and crises. In particular, the school has been met with various identity concerns and problems over the years that have included controversy associated with the university's athletic program.

In less than a decade, Baylor experienced a monumental rise: a tremendous win-loss record, a highly prolific offenses scheme, and the recruitment of highly sought after players that proved to be college stars and NFL players.

However, just when it appeared that the Baylor Bears football program and its unabashed leader, Coach Briles, was on the cusp of being a perennial college football powerhouse, an unholy scandal emerged in Waco. There were rumblings of improprieties within the school's athletic department and specifically ones that implicated the football program and its head coach. The investigation and the troubling details left the institution without a football coach, an athletic director, and a university president.

Penn State. The child sex abuse scandal that rocked Penn State in 2011 shed light on the reality that a revered and beloved football coach, Joe Paterno, was at least partially responsible for the abuse of several boys over several years because he neglected to report his friend and assistant coach, Jerry Sandusky, to the police after Paterno was told by an eyewitness that Sandusky had raped a boy in the shower. In 2011, a grand jury report was released, detailing Sandusky's widespread abuse of boys he met through his own charitable organization. Just days after the report was released, Sandusky was arraigned on 40 criminal counts and the Penn State president and Joe Paterno were fired ("Penn State Scandal Fast Facts," 2016).

The Cardinal Sins in the 'Ville. In 2015, the University of Louisville Cardinals basketball program was rocked by allegations of various salacious activities going on within the program. Details of strippers, escorts, and sex parties were reported in the tell-all *Breaking Cardinal Rules: Basketball and the Escort Queen* by Katina Powell. The scandal brought much unwanted attention—as well as a NCAA investigation—to UL. The team suffered a self-imposed ban on postseason play at the end of the 2015–2016 season as well as further NCAA sanctions.

Lance and Tiger. The idea of the public behavior of athletes being a reflection of the reputation of the teams they represent is commonly understood, but in many cases, there are athletes who stand apart from teams or compete alone. Still, the behavior of these athletes affects not only the athletes but other companies associated with them as well.

Tiger. On November 27, 2009, when Tiger Woods crashed his Cadillac Escalade into a fire hydrant very close to his home, the event marked the beginning of the freefall of Tiger Woods' public image. The sex scandal that ensued resulted in fans finding out that Woods had repeatedly cheated on his wife. By the end of 2010, Woods was divorced, his Q Score was the lowest it had ever been, and he was losing endorsement deals, including Gatorade, AT&T, Accenture and Tag Heuer. The Associated Press estimated that between 2009 and 2010, Woods had lost $22 million in endorsement deals (Wei, 2010). Nike, however, did not waver in its support of Woods.

Lance. In October 2012, the United States Anti-Doping Agency (USADA) released a 212-page report that revealed professional cyclist and 7-time Tour de France winner Lance Armstrong was at the center of "a massive team doping scheme, more extensive than any previously revealed in professional sports history" (Albergotti

& O'Connell, 2013). Armstrong was stripped of his seven victories and was banned for life from professional cycling. He also lost endorsement deals with Anheuser-Busch and Nike.

While these two sport scandals were both explosive and did untold damage to Woods and Armstrong, Nike's decision to continue supporting Woods while quickly disassociating itself from Armstrong actually provides a clear example of Nike's brand identity: its belief in sport. Woods cheated, but he cheated in his personal life. Armstrong cheated, but he cheated in his role as an athlete, and to Nike, that is the difference between endorsing and firing.

While public behavior, particularly the behavior of professional athletes, is the most difficult of the brand identity elements to manage directly, the ones that remain are fairly easily managed with a great measure of control and consistency.

"Deflategate." You could not live in New England during 2015 and 2016 without hearing references to deflated footballs and accusations that the New England Patriots had cheated in their January 18, 2015, AFC Championship victory over the Indianapolis Colts. The Patriots were accused of exchanging the first half's 12 game balls with a new set of 12 slightly deflated balls. When all was said and done nearly two years later, the New England Patriots paid a $1 million fine, gave up two draft picks—a first-round in 2016 and a fourth-round in 2017—and Tom Brady served a four-game suspension after unsuccessfully appealing it to the 2nd U.S. Circuit Court of Appeals ("Deflategate Timeline: After 544 days, Tom Brady Gives in," 2016).

Jared the "Creepy Subway Guy." Subway is a preeminent example of a company that markets its brand through sport sponsorship. Jared Fogle became an official spokesperson for the sandwich juggernaut in 2000 after he experienced significant weight loss through a combination of exercise and the calorie-conscious Subway sandwich diet (Wallace-McRee, In Press). Jared personified Subway's desired brand attributes because he demonstrated the benefits associated with major weight loss. He conducted personal appearances and took part in various other marketing endeavors for the company. However, after years of association with the company, Jared's story turned from inspiration to repulsion as the company's pitchman was embroiled in a major sex scandal involving children and child pornography. After the story broke, Subway was quick to scrub the image of "Jared the Subway Guy" from its website and other company touchpoints (Wallace-McRee, In Press).

REI Closes for Black Friday. Not all behaviors are negative. Recreational Equipment, Inc., better known as REI, is a leading outdoor recreation retail corporation. This company, which sells products geared toward outdoor pursuits, has been able to provide differentiation due to the practice of closing its stores on "Black Friday" in recent years. This practice—this behavior—has served to send a strong marketing message that has become part of the company's brand identity.

Conclusion

Actions and behaviors—both positive and negative—influence the perceptions and ultimately the engagement of stakeholders and other audiences, so organizations need to be mindful of the ramifications of personal actions (or lack thereof) and behaviors. Communicating and controlling a strong brand identity is important, but it can be particularly difficult to control the collective and individual actions of organizational participants, employees, and other stakeholders.

This chapter provides exemplars of scandals and controversies to shed light on the effects of negative behavior. While some situations may be more detrimental than others, it is important that sport organizations consider their behavior as an integral part of their brand identity management.

Part 2

Communicating the Brand Identity

Chapter 7

Touchpoints

A brand touchpoint refers to each and every opportunity a stakeholder has to interact with the brand identity. This chapter focuses on any and all brand touchpoints, whether strategic or opportunistic. Strategic touchpoints are those generated or manufactured by the brand itself, such as official social media sites, advertising, signage and licensed apparel, among others. Because they are generated by the organization itself, strategic touchpoints are positive and are meant to promote the brand identity with the intention of reinforcing a positive image in the minds of stakeholders and the general public. Conversely, opportunistic touchpoints are those generated by members of the fan base, rivals or other stakeholders, and these are created without the knowledge or permission of the organization. These touchpoints may include negative touchpoints, such as "suck sites," unlicensed apparel and unofficial social media pages. These touchpoints can vary widely in the sport context. Because they may be created either by fans or rivals, organizations run the risk of having to contend with negative opportunistic touchpoints, and in some cases, trademark or copyright infringement, which will be discussed in a later chapter.

This chapter will focus on discussions of the major strategic touchpoints that most sport organizations employ, as well as a discussion of some opportunistic touchpoints that have reflected both positively and negatively on their targeted organizations.

Advertising

Advertising is recognized by its purpose of influencing, informing, persuading, communicating, and dramatizing messages desiring to convey a convincing identity for institutions (Wheeler, 2006). While there are a variety of different definitions available, they generally have a few elements in common: advertising is paid, nonpersonal, has an identified sponsor, is disseminated through the mass media, and it is intended to persuade or influence.

Higher education institutions devote great effort and expense to institutional advertising as part of the university marketing initiatives (Harris, 2009). Advertising can serve as an impactful component of a university's brand identity touchpoints in a variety of ways aimed at reaching relevant publics and various other stakeholders (e.g., by persuading future potential students to enroll and by informing stakeholders of innovation, scholarly excellence, or athletic success).

The University of Alabama's "Where Legends Are Made" Campaign. The "Where Legends Are Made" campaign was a unique branding campaign unveiled during the national broadcast of the University of Alabama Crimson Tide football game versus the University of Southern California Trojans during the opening week of major college football in 2016 (Lee, Vincent & Hull, Under Development). This innovative advertising campaign sent a strong message attesting to the University of Alabama's penchant for producing success stories in both athletics and academics. The "Where Legends Are Made" tagline has been used in various campaign touchpoints, including print ads, billboards and other signage, website and social media communications, assorted business communication forms (e.g., letterhead/stationery) and branded merchandise.

Orangetheory Fitness. Orangetheory Fitness, an interval training center, has implemented the unique and highly non-traditional marketing practice of placing orange bicycles in strategic places. This "guerilla marketing" tactic is aimed at generating buzz while increasing word-of-mouth (WOM) for the company.

Sport Organization and Team Websites

Organizational Websites. Every sport organization has various promotional tools available at their disposal. Marketing through Web sites provides an easy way to convey messages to intended publics, as well as a dynamic way to communicate the organization's brand identity. The reality of having just a presence on the Web, however, has evolved into the need for a social media presence.

Social Media. Social media is composed of online websites and tools that encourage user interaction through creating, sharing, and publishing content (Nassar, 2012). Social media provides organizations the opportunity to establish relationships with stakeholders by enabling "one-to-one" interactions in which the organization can present information and receive regular feedback from stakeholders (Aggarwal, 2009; Hussain & Ferdous, 2015).

Furthermore, the emergence of social media—Facebook, Instagram, Twitter, YouTube, Snapchat, Pinterest, etc.—has amplified the potential for internet-based communication by allowing organizations to communicate messages directly to their target audiences. Most importantly, Websites and social media touchpoints are often the first source sought out by stakeholders for information on an organization, so it is imperative that the social media channels reflect the true voice and brand identity of the organization.

MSU. Mississippi State University's athletic department has employed various social media communication cues to elicit a response with stakeholders. Examples of this include the use of @HailState for the athletic department's Twitter and Instagram handles and the #HailState hashtag for social media communications. In addition to the #HailState hashtag, the university made use of a modified hashtag—"#Ha1lState"—when the university's football team was ranked first in the country during the 2014 season. Other social media designations have been used, including #CLANGA, which pays homage to MSU's beloved cowbell and the noise these instruments make.

#Htowntakeover. By maximizing social media practices and content, the University of Houston has been able to make great progress toward their institutional marketing goals. Recently, the school decided to position itself on social media by using the H-Town Takeover campaign. The H-Town Takeover campaign has become a rallying point for the University of Houston faithful. It is deployed through various channels and includes the #HTown-Takeover hashtag on social media communications. The school has even used this as the name on its official Twitter account. By employing focused social media marketing campaigns, the University of Houston Cougars' athletics has been able to send strong messages that resonate with stakeholders (Hull, Lee & Zapalac, In Progress).

#FreeUAB. In the aftermath of the decision to eliminate the football program at the University of Alabama at Birmingham, various stakeholders decided to take to social media sites to engage the public on the topic, taking a page from the recent rules of crisis communication. The creators of the sites wanted to express their disappointment and anger over the decision while also engaging others who feel the same. The #FreeUAB hashtag became a rallying cry that connected social media users to the cause. This hashtag was not a strategic effort developed by the institution but was enacted by passionate fans (important stakeholders) and social media users to bring attention to what they viewed as an injustice.

Atlanta Hawks. The NBA's Atlanta Hawks (@ATLHawks) organization uses its Twitter feed to provide witty and clever game commentary with an added mixture of popular culture images and gifs. The organization has also shown a penchant for dialogue by interacting with other teams in the league (something that many NBA teams do very well). An example of Atlanta's innovative Twitter strategy occurred in January of 2015; the Atlanta Hawks went on an improbable 18-game winning streak. One of the ways they celebrated this streak was by adding a "W" to its "Hawks" Twitter name for each win. In February, when the streak ended, the team changed its name to "Fun while it lasted!" (Watkins, In Press).

Transit

Many sport organizations may choose to promote their programs or events using traditional transit advertising, such as ads on local buses and bus shelters as well as in and around the subway and location stations. Transit advertising is an effective way to reach a localized audience in a way that is quick to produce and relatively inexpensive.

Vehicles can also provide an important role by serving as traveling branding tools (Alessandri, 2009; Wheeler, 2006). Such advertisements can occur on a wide assortment of vehicle types: cars, vans, work trucks, mass transit (Bernstein, 1997). Organizations seeking to use vehicles as branding tools need to be mindful of the messages that are conveyed as they travel on the roads, or through the air or water. Organizations also need to understand that the manner in which these vehicles are maintained and operated provide opportunities for brand associations, as well.

Generally speaking, it is important to follow the rules of good signage and consider the issues of visibility, legibility, positioning, and durability. For example, consider the messages that may be conveyed if the vehicle is in poor condition or if individuals operating the branded vehicles are driving in an aggressive or erratic manner.

Some sport organizations may charter motorcoaches or jets to get their teams from one location to another. Those charters, particularly buses that are left at a sport venue, become de facto touchpoints for the sport organization.

Crystal Palace. In London, the Premier League's Crystal Palace Football Club was set to play the Middlesbrough Football Club. The teams woke on the morning of the match to find a motorcoach vandalized by Crystal Palace fans. It was easy to figure who vandalized the bus because they had written "Crystal Palace FC" in spray paint along the length of the coach. The fans presumably meant to vandalize the Middlesbrough bus as a show of loyalty and perhaps aggression. What they failed to realize is that Middlesbrough had flown to the match and had borrowed one of the Crystal Palace team coaches. In the end, the fans vandalized their own teams' equipment (Curtis, 2017).

Boston Red Sox "Truck Day." In what has become known as New England's version of Groundhog Day, each February Red Sox fans brave the early morning cold—and often snow—to stand outside Fenway Park and watch as movers load a 53-foot truck with equipment for the two-day drive to spring training in Florida. In 2016, the tractor trailer included 20,400 baseballs, 1,100 bats, 200 pairs of batting gloves and helmets, 300 pairs of pants and 60 cases of sunflower seeds (Cole, 2016). This tradition, known as Truck Day, has evolved from an anonymous job into a rite of near spring, with press and fans mingling with Wally the Green Monster (in a Hawaiian shirt), enjoying local university bands and Dunkin Donuts giveaways (Healey, 2014). Fans watch as the branded truck—emblazoned with quotes such as "On the Road to Greatness," "The Green Monster's On the Move," and "With the Sox For the Long Haul"—takes to the road toward warmer weather and Opening Day.

Specialty Branded Vehicles. In some cases, a sport organization will invest tremendous resources in a specialty vehicle emblazoned with one or more elements of its brand identity. The vehicle is limited neither to four wheels or to the ground: it may be a car, truck, bus, plane or helicopter—or even a blimp.

Giving You Wings—Or Rotors. Red Bull maintains a large fleet of small cars that it deploys as part of its ambassador force, a group of people in large cities who give out samples and generally act as goodwill ambassadors and brand champions. The cars are small passenger vehicles with a large replica of a Red Bull can on top. As the brand has gotten more closely aligned with extreme sports, its investment in promoting its brand identity has increased with the acquisition of a helicopter. It provided support and some fairly exciting brand identity promotion during the making of a Red Bull film about extreme freestyle snowboarding, "The Art of Flight."

The Goodyear Blimp. In this modern area of sport, perhaps the most famous specialty branded vehicle is the Goodyear Blimp. The fleet of three airships and blimps fly above live sporting events and provide aerial coverage. In the early 2000s, when high-definition television was just becoming mainstream, the *Spirit of Goodyear* became the first blimp to provide high-definition live video to a national sports event (Relive History, 2017).

Professional Cycling's Team Buses. Professional cyclists who spend their careers racing hundreds of miles each week also spend a lot of time on their team buses getting from stage to stage during the races. These team buses act as rolling billboards for the teams, many of which are named after their corporate sponsors. British-based Team Sky has a bus commonly referred to as the "Death Star." It is a sleek, large black bus—complete with a movie screen, kitchen, shower and assigned seats for each of the riders—emblazoned with the "Team Sky" name, with Sky written in its exclusive corporate typeface.

Signage. "Signage is a mass communication medium that works 24 hours a day, and helps people identify, navigate, and understand the environment" (Hussain & Ferdous, 2015, p. XX). Signage provides brand-building opportunities, as they can be impactful in articulating and invigorating identity (Hussain & Ferdous, 2015). Signage should be easily visible and send both a clear and compelling message. Successful signage implementation needs to effectively address the issues of visibility, legibility, positioning, and durability to maximize the process (Wheeler, 2006). Signs should also include easily identifiable elements of the organization's brand identity touchpoints.

Swag → Athletic Ephemera. Marketing ephemera refers to a wide variety of marketing items that have one thing in common: a short lifespan. Organizations commonly use ephemera for marketing and promotion activities at trade shows, expos, and events. Ephemera in the form of "swag" items are a staple at athletic events across all levels and on game days or before. Such items, because they are often free, provide useful and positive public relations that can convey messages such as "think of us," "see what we are doing," or "thank you" (Wheeler, 2006).

Typical ephemera includes such items as pens, highlighters, pins, mugs, caps, t-shirts, bags, folders, USB memory sticks, notebooks and more to convey the organization's message.

Premiums and Promotional Giveaways. In sport, like many other aspects of life, fans prefer giveaways, particularly ones that are related in some way to the event/organization (Dick & Turner, 2007). Consider going to a baseball game where organizers give away items such as mini bats or caps or even bobbleheads. Such items are attractive for a variety of reasons, including that they are tangible items that fuel positive feelings and associations with the experience (Wakefield, 2016).

Fetchko, Roy, and Clow (2013) identify two types of sales promotions: 1) ones that encourage the audience to take action by reducing risk and 2) those that provide incentives by adding value for consumers. Sales promotions that reduce risk do so by removing barriers that might deter individuals from trying or using products. This can include product samples or coupons. Sales promotions are promotional endeavors that can add value for customers by giving consumers added benefits for attending and for the price paid. "Premium" is the term applied to sales promotions that add such value by providing consumers items of value—such as gift items or apparel—when attending events or purchasing products.

Giveaways at sporting events are able to add value to promotional activities. For example, giving away t-shirts to attendees at "color-out" games serve the purpose of having fans wearing the home team colors. This practice allows for fans to feel they are part of the game, are able to take part in a meaningful demonstration of fanship, and they come away with a souvenir that allows them to demonstrate team pride any other time they wear that shirt in the future (Wakefield, 2016).

Conclusion

This chapter discussed the deployment of a sport organization's brand identity. That is, how an organization uses its brand identity elements across media to promote it and the organization. These media, called touchpoints, can range from traditional marketing materials, such as advertising, publicity, and social media, to more non-traditional elements, such as vehicles. Finally, one tactic that has been used widely in sport at all levels is ephemera such as sales promotion, premiums and other giveaways.

Part 3

Protecting and Exploiting the Brand Identity

Chapter 8

Trademarks and Licensing

Any licensing agreement starts with a trademark. In 1947, the federal government began providing widespread protection for the individual and collective elements of an organization's brand identity—names, logos, taglines and color palettes—through trademark law. Although trademark law had existed for a long time in common law form at the state level, federal trademark law was codified in the Lanham Act. The Lanham Act defines a trademark as "any word, name, symbol, or device" that identifies or distinguishes the source of goods or services. The law also recognizes "trade dress," or the unified look of an organization, which means that there is legal protection available for a sensory branding approach that employs sounds, scents, and color.

Once an organization has a trademark, it is incumbent upon that organization to protect the mark, and the most basic way is to use the proper trademark symbol alongside the trademarked term or symbol. For example, use of the ™ symbol communicates that the trademark in question is relatively new, or at least that it has not reached registered trademark status. This ™ symbol can be used any time after the development of the trademark itself. Although it does not carry full legal weight, use of the ™ symbol communicates to the general public that the organization is claiming rights in the mark. It is a sort of placeholder while the organization seeks the "holy grail" of protection: officially registered trademark status. Once trademarks have gone through the required lengthy legal process and finally reached registered trademark status, they have earned the right—and the responsibility—to use the ® symbol. Legally speaking, use of this symbol serves as "constructive notice" of the organization's trademark. Practically speaking, appropriate deployment of the symbol will aid in reaping financial damages if a trademark infringement case ever finds its way to court (Wilson, 1998).

Exploiting a Trademark Through Licensing. When a sport organization has a loyal fan base or a winning team—or both—the trademarks of that organization become ever more valuable. And valuable trademarks—from names to logos to colors—can translate into a robust licensing program, a profitable extra revenue stream for the organization.

Licensing agreements refer to a trademark owner allowing a vendor to apply the trademark to anything from apparel or furniture to toys in exchange for a fee, and typically a percentage of the proceeds. Licensing agreements are pervasive in sport, and fans need walk no further than the gift shop at an arena or stadium—or into the college bookstore—to see evidence of this. For example, Collegiate Licensing Company (CLC) is the major player in the collegiate licensing industry and partners with nearly 200 colleges, universities, athletic conferences, bowl games, the Heisman Trophy and the NCAA. CLC handles all of the details of the organization's' licensing program by vetting license candidates and managing the royalties, which range from 10 to 15 percent in a standard case (CLC.com, 2017).

The value of licensing is represented by the 3P Model. The 3Ps of licensing refer to *profit*, *promotion*, and *protection*. In essence, licensors are able to generate revenue streams by licensing out their intellectual property (*profit*). Furthermore, intellectual property rights holders can benefit from the promotion of their images and symbols through the presence of licensed products that range from the commonplace (i.e., t-shirts) to the obscure (i.e., corn on the cob holders) (*promotion*). At the same time, licensors are able to help ensure quality control through licensing agreements (*protection*). In this sense, they are able to protect their intellectual property rights.

A trademark provides important legal protection for one or more elements of a brand identity, and, if marketed, licensed and protected properly, the trademark will continue to pay dividends to the organization.

Before an element of the brand's identity can become a trademark, however, it must meet at least a minimum threshold of originality, and not every popular mark is deemed fit for trademark status.

BOSTON STRONG but not Trademark Strong. On Monday, April 15, 2013, just hours after terrorists detonated two bombs at the finish line of the Boston Marathon, two Boston college students created the phrase, "Boston Strong," which would become the rallying cry for a healing city. Just two days later, two different people tried to trademark that very phrase.

"Boston Strong" was written in yellow block letters against a royal blue background. The colors were an obvious choice—the Boston Athletic Association, organizer of the Boston Marathon, has long used blue and yellow in its logo and promotional materials. The students admit that the simple phrase that would be heard and used by citizens and world leaders alike—Boston Strong—was not a flash of their creative genius, but a phrase that has crept into our collective consciousness over the past decade. "We developed Boston Strong off of Livestrong and Army Strong because it was something simple people could get behind" (Zimmer, 2013).

While the college students had really only hoped to raise some money for the victims, Boston Strong quickly became "a handy shorthand for defiance, solidarity, and caring" (Zimmer, 2013). On April 16, Red Sox third baseman Will Middlebrooks tweeted: "I can't wait to put on my jersey today … I get to play for the strongest city out there. #BostonStrong." At the Boston Bruins first game after the bombing, on April 17, the team superimposed a blue and yellow "Boston Strong" ribbon on the home ice.

Elsewhere around the city on April 17, two individuals prepared trademark applications for "Boston Strong." According to the United States Patent and Trademark Office (USPTO) records, one applicant applied as an individual for the exclusive right to use "Boston Strong" on "imprinting T-shirts; Imprinting messages on wearing apparel, accessories, and mugs; Imprinting of decorative designs on T-shirts." By April 25, however, the application was withdrawn.

The second applicant applied for the exclusive right to use "Boston Strong" on "clothing and accessories." The second applicant owned a company that sells Boston sports merchandise online. He told *The Huffington Post* that his motives weren't commercial but protective:

> "he was concerned that someone outside the Boston area would try to enforce the trademark. 'Our interest isn't to police the mark,' he said. 'It's more to indemnify and protect ourselves and our colleagues and partners'" (Dicker, 2013).

Trademark experts recognize the issue immediately: the applicant's assertion that he would not police the mark goes against everything trademark law is meant to provide: exclusivity. Meanwhile, the creators of Boston Strong had managed to collect thousands of followers on their Facebook page, and were adhering to—and promoting—their initial assertion that "Boston Strong" was not meant to be a commercial endeavor, but one that would help to bring some sort of benefit to the victims and the city alike.

As of July 11, 2013, the USPTO had received 10 trademark applications for "Boston Strong," including the one withdrawn by the first applicant. The applicants requested the exclusive use of "Boston Strong" on everything from clothing to jewelry, coffee, and beer. One applicant requested the use of bostonstrong.com to raise funds for a variety of disaster relief programs. On July 15, the USPTO issued a stern rejection of four of the trademark applications:

> Consumers are accustomed to seeing this motto or slogan used with respect to the marathon bombing, sporting events, as well as on a variety of consumer goods ... An applicant may not overcome this refusal by attempting to amend the application ... to assert claim of acquired distinctiveness. (Davis, 2013)

Once granted a trademark, an organization that does not vigilantly protect its trademarks may be confronted by one of any number of threats—infringement, dilution, and counterfeiting.

Infringement

Owning a registered trademark provides basic legal protection from infringement, but trademark owners must be able to prove that use of a similar mark, presumably by a competitor, is likely to confuse consumers by making them believe that the product with the infringed trademark is actually a product of the trademark owner. Proving infringement, however, is not as simple as claiming the use of a trademark that is too similar to the original. The courts use a lengthy list of criteria to determine if there is a "likelihood of confusion" in the marketplace.

To determine if a trademark is likely to cause confusion, the court would weigh eight factors: 1) the strength of the plaintiff's trademark, 2) the similarity of the plaintiff's and defendant's trademarks, 3) the similarity of the two organization's trade channels, 4) the similarity of the goods offered by the two organizations, 5) the sophistication of the market's buyers, 6) the degree of care likely to be exercised by the consumers during their purchase, 7) the issue of bridging the gap—whether the plaintiff crosses over into areas of business currently served by the defendant, and 8) the geographic extent of the trade channels served by the plaintiff and defendant (*Polaroid Corp. v. Polarad Elect. Corp.*, 287 F.2d 492 (2d Cir. 1961)).

Local Little League teams and town soccer teams have longed adopted the names of well-known college and professional sports teams as their own, perhaps paying tribute to the teams or offering their school-age players the chance to emulate their favorite players. While the use of these teams' trademarks is a case of infringement, there has been little to no enforcement on the local level. Little League, itself a trademarked term, provides rather interesting guidance on the use of Major League Baseball trademarks. In summary, Little League believes in the protection of its own trademarks, but supports using the registered trademarks of Major

League Baseball even if doing so results in an infringement action against another vendor:

> For more than six decades, Little Leagues have used the names of Major League Baseball teams. Major League Baseball has never restricted any Little League teams from calling themselves "Mets," "Yankees," "Cardinals," "Angels," or any of its other trademarked names.
>
> However, we also recognize the importance to Major League Baseball of the protection of its trademarks. It is incumbent on any organization, Little League included, to protect its trademarks. To fail to do so can result in those valuable trademarks being lost.
>
> We strongly encourage our leagues who wish to place any trademarked names on a uniform item, including those of Major League Baseball clubs, to use only those items authorized and licensed by Major League Baseball.
>
> It is important to note that unauthorized use of any trademark, including those belonging to Major League Baseball, may result in civil liability by the manufacturer of items bearing those trademarks. So, even though a local Little League that uses shirts with unauthorized Major League Baseball trademarks will not be held liable, it is likely that the business that provided the shirts would be. (Use of Third Party Trademarked Names and Logos, 2017).

While the MLB has tacitly approved of Little League's use of its trademarks, other college and professional sport organizations have begun to push back on high school teams, particularly as high school athletes begin to earn television time formerly only awarded to college and professional athletes.

Glades Day School, a 390-student private school in Belle Glade, Florida, adopted Gators as the school's teams' name and mascot when the school was founded in 1965. Although the school's logo was green and gold, in most other respects it was identical to the Gator logo of the University of Florida. The nearly identical logo was presumably unknown to the University of Florida until Glades Day School went to the state championship and was featured on television in late 2009. In 2010, the University of Florida demanded that Glades Day cease and desist in using the university's trademarks and, in the process, change its name and mascot. The school's headmaster, who himself was a University of Florida alumnus, agreed to make the required changes rather than face the possibility of exorbitant legal fees, but he told the *New York Times:* "It just hurts. It has a sting to it. We send them our students, we send them our money and we support them. It just flies in the face of common sense that they would come after us" (Himmelsbach, 2010).

Trademark owners, as well as those in the licensing or merchandising industries, would disagree. Colleges and universities are necessarily vigilant about protecting their trademarks because they are well aware of the revenue that derives from those marks through licensing agreements.

Woo Pig Suit-ee. The University of Arkansas brought a trademark infringement action against an independent physical therapy clinic for trademark infringement when the clinic owners renamed their clinic "Razorback Sport and Physical Therapy" (*Trustees Univ. of Ark. v. Professional Therapy Serv.,* 873 F. Supp. 1280 (W.D. Ark. 1995)). Though the clinic was founded in 1971, it changed its name in 1988 in an effort to be more marketable. The new name referenced the "Razorback" name belonging to the University of Arkansas, and that was unacceptable to the university. The name Razorback and the associated images were clearly similar to the University of Arkansas at Fayetteville's trademarks. Also, the university thought there was potential for additional confusion because the proprietors of the clinic were the former Director of Sports Medicine at the university and a current university trainer. To make matters worse, Razorback Sports and Physical Therapy advertised and promoted its relationship to the university. The judge ruled that the University of Arkansas marks and those of the clinic were similar. Additionally, the judge found that the Razorback mark clearly symbolized the university, the clinic and the university offered competitive services, and there was reason to believe there could be confusion among the public.

Dilution

As early as 1927, two decades before the Lanham Act granted trademark owners protection from trademark infringement, Schechter (1927) warned that trademarks were being diluted—that is, the power of their message was being "whittled away" by competitors in *other* markets:

> Trademark pirates are growing more subtle and refined. They proceed circumspectly, by suggestion and approximation, rather than by direct and exact duplication of their victims' wares and marks. The history of important trademark litigation within recent years shows that the use of similar marks on *non*-competing goods is perhaps the *normal* rather than the exceptional case of infringement (Schechter, 1927).

Unlike trademark infringement, in which the courts use a standard of confusion in the consumer marketplace, dilution is viewed as the use of a trademark that is simply similar to an established "famous" mark and likely to dilute the power of the original mark. In theory, proving dilution of a trademark means a lower bar for trademark owners in that no proof of consumer confusion is necessary, but the mark must be deemed famous to enjoy this level of protection. In reality, however, since the federal law against trademark dilution was enacted in the mid-1990s, courts have had a difficult time defining what dilution actually is (Farley, 2006).

Counterfeiting

Perhaps even more than infringement and dilution, trademark owners with the most famous athletic programs need to be concerned about predators making an illegal end-run around licensing agreements by counterfeiting trademarks for pure profit.

According to the Trademark Counterfeiting Act of 1984 (15 USC §1127), Congress defined a counterfeit trademark as a phony trademark used in connection with trafficked goods or services that are identical to, or indistinguishable from, an actual registered trademark for those goods or services. The counterfeit mark must be likely to cause confusion, mistake, or deception (Goldstone & Toren, 1998).

Due to the immense popularity of collegiate apparel, counterfeiters see opportunity. In fact, the market for licensed collegiate apparel is, quite simply, a behemoth of a business that brings in about $4.3 billion annually (Dosh, 2012), so counterfeiters can skim off the top and still not make a major dent in the market demand for branded goods.

In 2011, more than 60,000 pieces of counterfeit clothing and apparel featuring collegiate trademarks were seized by the Collegiate Licensing Company. The estimated face value of the counterfeit goods was more than $1 million (Dosh, 2012).

The most opportunistic counterfeiters, however, choose the high holidays of collegiate sport—the national championships—to hawk their wares. Collegiate Licensing Company reports that approximately 5,000 counterfeit items are seized annually outside the stadium where the national football championship game is played (Dosh, 2012).

When it comes to collegiate athletics, fans and counterfeiters might take a more proprietary view: it's *their* team and they want to pay tribute. So rather than seeing their unauthorized use of trademarks as a violation, many counterfeiters—notwithstanding their personal financial gain—might believe they are paying homage to their favorite team.

Perhaps an important caveat here is this: many fans may not care that an apparel item is technically and legally counterfeit if it appears to be "official" in its use of names, logos, and colors, so sales of counterfeit items can be brisk. It is the same mindset that drives sales of counterfeit luxury items: if the fake looks real, why not save money by forgoing the original brand?

Imitation ≠ Flattery

There are significant revenues at stake in a licensing deal, yet colleges and universities understand that "official merchandise" endorsed by a licensing agent such as CLC is not always a consumer requirement. For this reason, colleges and universities have recently become much more vigilant about protecting their trademarks from encroachment beyond the traditional forms of infringement and counterfeiting.

Many protective efforts are now aimed at secondary schools using exact replicas of collegiate trademarks, as was the case between the University of Florida and Glades Day School. Schools have also become more aware of the power of singular elements of their brand identities, such as color, and have begun protecting those in isolation.

Smack Apparel. Tampa, Florida-based Smack Apparel was founded in 1998 and manufactures and sells fan merchandise that deliberately draws upon the associations between universities and their colors. The company does this without a licensing agreement with the schools, stating prominently on its Web site that Smack is "Licensed only by the First Amendment." Smack makes a somewhat illogical argument for its belief that it can do business without legal license agreements: "It's not that we are averse to being licensed; we are just averse to the CREATIVE RESTRICTION that would come along with being licensed" (www.smackapparel.com).

But that "creative restriction" Smack Apparel opposes is, of course, the very reason for licensing: it allows the trademark owner to ensure the integrity of the brand identity, both in terms of the colors, typefaces, and logos, but also the appropriateness of the treatment.

Louisiana State University, University of Oklahoma, Ohio State University and the University of Southern California experienced major issues with Smack's use of its brand identities and were undeterred by the company's reference to the First Amendment. The four universities joined forces and sued Smack Apparel for selling t-shirts in the respective colors of their universities along with associated facts and indicia, such as landmark game scores. For example, one t-shirt in USC's cardinal and gold colors cited by the plaintiffs included the saying: "Got eight?" on the front and "Home of the 8 Time National Champions" on the back. It also included an outline of the state of California, with "SoCal" marked on it. Another shirt in LSU's purple and gold, referencing the Sugar Bowl, had "Bourbon Street or Bust" on the front with the "ou" in "Bourbon" in a different typeface, presumably referencing the University of Oklahoma. The back included the phrase, "Show us your beads!" with the "ou" in "your" in a different typeface and the phrase "Sweet as Sugar" (Board of Supervisors for Louisiana State University Agricultural and Mechanical College v. Smack Apparel Co., 2008).

While both the district and appeals courts ruled in the plaintiff's favor, Smack Apparel continues to produce college and professional sport apparel, but with references limited to the school's geography, colors, and primary competitors. For example, a University of North Carolina at Chapel Hill fan would go to the Smack Apparel Web site and search for "Chapel Hill," which will bring fans to several t-shirts. Each shirt is the trademark Carolina Blue. In one example, a Carolina Blue baby onesie, reads: "Is it just me or does Duke stink?"

In a case of a pre-emptive change in light of a potential trademark infringement action, the NFL's Jacksonville Jaguars franchise selected the name Jaguars and unveiled the initial team logo and found itself embroiled in controversy because the logo was deemed too similar to that of the Jaguar automobile manufacturer. After designing a new logo, the team was able to market the logo and team's associated color palette of teal, black, and white, with a secondary color of gold (Lee & Sweeney, 2011).

Tattoo You. Major sports fans often choose to display their loyalty to their favorite team by tattooing the name or logo of that team on their bodies. There is surprisingly little information from the major sports leagues on this very issue, which is likely due to the fact that the teams and the leagues do not want to deter their most loyal fans from expressing their love for their teams. The question does arise, however, and so a blogger for *The Straight Dope* contacted four of the major professional sports leagues—

Major League Baseball, the National Basketball Association, the National Football League and the National Hockey League—to seek some guidance. The only league that responded to the request was Major League Baseball, which didn't provide much guidance at all:

> Any use of MLB or Club trademarks requires assessment of the nature and scope of the proposed use. We handle requests for use on a case by case basis and take action when it is discovered that these marks are used improperly ("Can I legally get myself tattooed with a pro sports team's logo?" 2011).

Slightly more guidance comes from the ever-vigilant International Olympic Committee. When asked by a blog whether athletes with tattoos faced the prospect of disqualification at the Olympic Games, an IOC spokesman responded:

> The IOC President is always excited to see athletes with the Olympic Rings. Standing alone, the Olympic Rings are a great expression of appreciation of the Olympic Games and of the Olympic Values (Pavitt, 2016).

Conclusion

This chapter has discussed the legal protection available to one or more elements of a sport organization's brand identity. Trademark law, officially known as the Lanham Act, provides legal protection against infringement, dilution, and counterfeiting. These protections are afforded to trademarks because the law understands that an exclusive trademark helps to identify a source of goods in the consumer marketplace, but also that a trademark is a business investment and one that, if protected, deserves to continue being an exclusive source of licensing revenue.

Conclusion

Closing the Loop: Practical Applications

A sport organization's brand identity is a practical tool with an incredible power. As a practical tool, a brand identity is a source of differentiation from competitors, other teams, and organizations. The brand identity includes the organization's name, logo, tagline, associated colors or an entire palette, and even the organization's architecture, interior design, and public behavior.

A brand identity has the ability to identify an organization, but it also has the power to help fans and stakeholders create positive associations with the organization. These associations are built over time, each time a stakeholder has an interaction with the brand identity on a number of different touchpoints. For this reason, it is imperative that a brand communicates in an integrated and consistent way: across media while using a singular message. This can be achieved if the brand employs a variety of touchpoints relevant to the organization.

Touchpoints are tangible business communication and marketing communication tactics that provide an interaction with a brand's stakeholders. Touchpoints can be any one of a number of business communication tactics (from business cards to letterhead) to traditional marketing tactics (advertising and social media) to non-traditional tactics such as vehicles and assorted giveaways.

This book has provided a thorough discussion of the elements of a sport organization's brand identity, as well as a plethora of examples of those elements as they are used in sport today.

This book also provides a discussion of how to protect an organization's brand identity through trademark law. Trademark law recognizes that a brand's name or logo, or even its colors, serve as identifiers in the marketplace, so the law protects them from infringement, dilution, and counterfeiting. Having a trademark in one or more elements of an identity can lead to profitable licensing programs, which refers to allowing a vendor to use a trademark (a license) on a variety of goods in exchange for a royalty.

The industry of sport—local, high school, college and professional—provides a fascinating context in which to study brand identity. This book was meant as both an introduction to the breadth of brand identity in the industry as well as a look at some of the examples that help illustrate how to both promote and protect the investment that brand identity represents. By no means does this book provide an exhaustive treatise on either the elements of brand identity nor best practices in the field. If there is an example you think should be included in future editions, please email one of the authors: Jason Lee at jason.lee@unf.edu or Susan Alessandri at salessandri@suffolk.edu.

Appendix 1

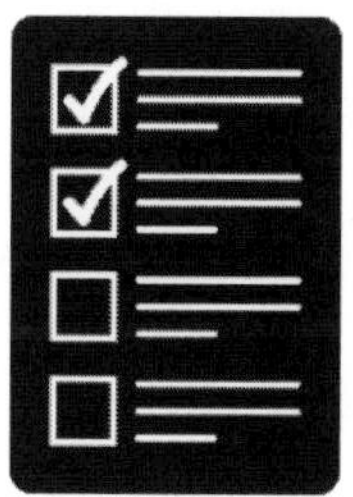

Visual (Brand) Identity Checklist

Organizational Stationery

- ❑ Letterhead
- ❑ Business cards
- ❑ Envelopes
- ❑ Checks
- ❑ Stock certificates
- ❑ Invoices
- ❑ Grant template
- ❑ Bill reminder
- ❑ Statements
- ❑ Purchase orders
- ❑ Contracts
- ❑ Memos
- ❑ Rubber stamps
- ❑ Proposals
- ❑ Presentation covers
- ❑ Luggage tags
- ❑ Note pads
- ❑ ID cards
- ❑ Security badges
- ❑ Embossing dies
- ❑ Organizational china

Digital/Electronic Displays

- ❑ Web sites
- ❑ Interactive kiosks
- ❑ Social media pages
- ❑ Voicemail
- ❑ News tickers
- ❑ Bulletin boards
- ❑ Online *Yellow Pages*
- ❑ Social Media sites
- ❑ Intranet
- ❑ Extranet
- ❑ Stock ticker symbol
- ❑ Blogs

Transportation

- ❑ Truck cab
- ❑ Pickup or van
- ❑ Trailer body
- ❑ Shipping containers
- ❑ Business car
- ❑ Airplanes
- ❑ Boats or ships
- ❑ Buses
- ❑ Freight car
- ❑ Parking lot decals
- ❑ Bumper stickers

Packing & Shipping

- ❑ Folding carton
- ❑ Labels
- ❑ Shipping tubes
- ❑ Tape
- ❑ Hang tags
- ❑ Mailing labels
- ❑ Gift boxes
- ❑ Cans
- ❑ Packing sheets
- ❑ Wrapping paper
- ❑ Stencils
- ❑ Shipping paper
- ❑ Decals
- ❑ Stamps
- ❑ Paper bags
- ❑ Package closures
- ❑ Meter postmark

Employee Communications

- ❑ Directory
- ❑ Newsletter
- ❑ Handbooks
- ❑ Paychecks

Architecture & Interior Design

- ❑ Exterior signage
- ❑ Exterior entrance
- ❑ Office name plates
- ❑ Retail store signage
- ❑ Interior lobby
- ❑ Interior design
- ❑ Interior entrance
- ❑ Landscaping
- ❑ Furniture
- ❑ Showrooms

Athletic Fields, Courts & Arenas

- ❑ Indoor courts
- ❑ Pool area
- ❑ Turf fields
- ❑ Golf courses
- ❑ Track
- ❑ Ice rink
- ❑ Bowling alley
- ❑ "Hall of Fame" area
- ❑ Locker rooms
- ❑ Locker room tunnels
- ❑ Scoreboard
- ❑ Pro shop
- ❑ Fan seating area
- ❑ Lobby area
- ❑ Baseball diamond

Marketing & Sales

- ❑ Sales manual
- ❑ Uniforms
- ❑ Audio visual
- ❑ Fliers
- ❑ Banner
- ❑ Window displays
- ❑ Shopping carts
- ❑ Info request sheets
- ❑ Fact sheets
- ❑ Catalog
- ❑ Pamphlets
- ❑ Newspaper ads
- ❑ Employment ads
- ❑ Ad insertion order
- ❑ Radio scripts
- ❑ Magazine ads
- ❑ Direct mail
- ❑ Posters
- ❑ Counter displays
- ❑ Contest materials
- ❑ Sales bulletins
- ❑ *Yellow Pages* ads
- ❑ Shopping carts
- ❑ Logo sheet
- ❑ TV ads
- ❑ Print ad formats
- ❑ Creative brief
- ❑ Co-op material
- ❑ Shelf talkers
- ❑ Spec sheets
- ❑ Promotions

Public Relations Materials

- ❑ Press kit folder
- ❑ Brochures
- ❑ Customer newsletters
- ❑ Media guides
- ❑ Podium identifier
- ❑ Team flags
- ❑ Brand identity manual
- ❑ Annual report
- ❑ Quarterly report
- ❑ Press release template

Apparel & Novelty Items

- ❑ Sweatshirts
- ❑ T-Shirts
- ❑ Sweatpants
- ❑ Baseball hats
- ❑ Souvenir postcards
- ❑ Lapel pins
- ❑ Baby toys
- ❑ Socks
- ❑ Baby clothing
- ❑ Stuffed animals
- ❑ Pennants
- ❑ Shopping bags
- ❑ Notebooks
- ❑ Pens/pencils
- ❑ Posters
- ❑ Tote bags

Appendix 2

Case in Point: Mississippi State University Visual Identity Examples

Name	The university goes by various monikers including "Mississippi State University," "MSU," and "Hail State" and the university's athletic programs are proudly known as the "Bulldogs."
The Colors	MSU's colors are Maroon and White. These colors have been in use for more than 100 years (Mississippi State Traditions, 2015).
Logos	MSU athletics incorporate a number of athletic "spirit marks," including the "M-State" mark (including an "M-State wordmark" variation), Bully (the Bulldog) marks, a "paw print" mark, and a cowbell mark (brand Identity Standards, 2015). MSU baseball also utilizes a "stacked MS" logo as well.
Mascots	The university employs multiple mascots including an American Kennel Club registered English Bulldog named "Bully" and a student wearing a Bulldog suit that also goes by the name "Bully" (Mississippi State Traditions, 2015).
The Cowbell	The cowbell is one of the most endearing and visible brand identity elements associated with MSU athletics. This is exemplified in the presence of the actual cowbells (and the associated clanging noise) and well as other brand elements (e.g., the cowbell logo) demonstrating the beloved cowbell.

Faces of the Program	The MSU Athletic Department has a number of notable individuals who have served as "faces" of the program. Specifically, the football program has a number of "faces"—most notably 2014 SEC Football Coach of the Year and Maxwell National Football Coach of the Year Dan Mullen (Dan Mullen Bio, 2015) and 2014 Heisman Candidate Quarterback Dak Prescott (Dak Prescott Bio, 2015).
Social Media Touchpoints	MSU's athletic department has utilized various social media communication cues to elicit a response with stakeholders. Examples of this include the use of @HailState for the athletic department's Twitter and Instagram handles and the #HailState hashtag for social media communications. With regard to the #HailState hashtag, the university also made use of a modified hashtag reference when the football team was ranked number 1 in the country in the 2014 season by incorporating the numeral "1" "#Ha1lState." Other social media designations have been used, including #CLANGA, which pays homage to the MSU stakeholder's beloved cowbell and the noise these instruments make.

Glossary

Visual (Brand) Vocabulary

The following terms provide further insight into issues presented in this book:

Aesthetic: A philosophical term referencing things which are pleasing to the senses (sight, sound, touch, feel, smell, taste).

Atmospherics: Characteristics and features such as venue scenery, sounds, smell, etc., which are associated with a sport and create a particular mood or attitude.

Brand: A brand is a blend of tangible and intangible attributes, which, if managed properly, creates distinction, influence, and value.

Brand Associations: The feelings, beliefs, and knowledge that consumers have about brands, which are derived from experiences and perceptions through time.

Brand Awareness: The degree to which consumers recognize and remember a brand.

Brand Personality: Attributing human personality traits (seriousness, warmth, imagination, etc.) to brands as a means of achieving differentiation and identification.

Licensing: A contractual agreement whereby an owner of intellectual property (e.g., trademarks) allows use to other parties in exchange for a royalty and/or a fee in a manner that transfers rights of use to another party without transferring of ownership.

Logo: A graphic mark used by brands for promotion, differentiation, and identification.

Mascot: A person, animal, or object used to represent a brand through association.

Positioning: Fixing a sport brand in the minds of the consumers based on its relevant position as compared to referent other brands.

Rebrand: A form of "brand transformation" that occurs when an owner or brand manager revisits the brand with the purpose of updating or revising attributes of the brand.

Stakeholders: Influential people with whom organizations wish to be affiliated.

Symbol: An object, picture, sound, word, or mark that is a representation through association.

Tagline: A memorable motto or phrase used by a brand for affiliation and recognition.

Trademark: A name, word, or symbol that identifies a brand from others in the marketplace. Trademarks are legally protected and are not be used without permission of the intellectual property owner.

Visual Identity: The strategically planned and purposeful presentation of a group, firm or organization. The identity is manifest in the organization's name, logo, tagline, color palette, architecture, interior design, public behavior, scents, sounds, etc.

References

1961. Polaroid Corporation v. Polarad Electronics Corporation. 287 F.2d 492.

Aaker, D. A. (1991). *Managing Brand Equity*. New York, NY: The Free Press.

About Charles Atlas (2016). Retrieved from http://charlesatlas.com/about.html

About Us. (2016). Retrieved from http://www.collegiatetartan.com/aboutus.asp

Aggarwal, A. (2009). Social Media strategies for hotels. Retrieved from http://www.hospitalitynet.org/news/4042853.html

Albergotti, R. & O'Connell, V. (2013). Behind Lance Armstrong's Decision to Talk. *Wall Street Journal*. Available online at: https://www.wsj.com/articles/SB10001424127887324734904578241801441261928. Accessed February 28, 2017.

Alessandri, S. W. (2009). *Visual Identity: Promoting and protecting the public face of an organization*. New York: M.E. Sharpe.

Alessandri, S.W. & Lee, J. W. (2016, December). Offensive high school mascots and community accountability. The Corporate Affairs, Reputation and Accountability Workshop at New York University's Stern School of Business, New York, NY.

Alessandri, S.W., Yang, S.U. & Kinsey, D.F. (2006). An integrative approach to university brand reputation. *Corporate Reputation Review*, *9*(4), 258–270. doi: 10.1057/palgrave.crr.1550033

Allianz Arena. (2017). Retrieved from http://www.colorkinetics.com/showcase/installs/Allianz-Arena/

The Art of Flight: The World's Most Progressive Snowboard Film. (2011). Available online at: https://www.redbull.tv/film/AP-1M7V16DXW2111/the-art-of-flight

Associated Press. (2001, May 23). NBA Blocks 'Express' as Name. Retrieved from http://articles.latimes.com/2001/may/23/sports/sp-1420

Babin, B. J. & Harris, W. G. (2012). *Consumer Behavior: CB3*. Mason, OH: Cengage Learning.

Baddeley, A. D. & Logie, R. H. (1999). Working memory: The multiple-component model. In A. Miyake & P. Shah (Eds.), *Models of working memory* (pp. 28–61). Cambridge: Cambridge University Press.

Balmer, J. M. T. & Liao, M. N. (2007). Student corporate brand identification: an exploratory case study. *Corporate Communications: An International Journal, 12*(4), 356–375. doi: 10.1108/13563280710832515

Benette, P. (2014). UofSC unveils its official tartan. Retrieved from http://www.sc.edu/uofsc/announcements/2014/03_tartan_unveiling.php#.WKif7mQrLu4

Bernstein, D. (1997). *Advertising Outdoors—Watch This Space!* London: Phaidon Press.

Berry, L. L. (2000). Cultivating service brand equity. *Journal of the Academy of Marketing Science, 28*(1), 128–137. doi: 10.1177/0092070300281012

Biel, A. L. (1993). Converting image into equity. In D. A. Aaker & A. L. Biel (Eds.), *Brand Equity and Advertising* (pp. 67–82). Hillsdale, NJ: Lawrence Erlbaum Associates.

Blue Cross Blue Shield of Oklahoma named title sponsor for Bedlam Series. (2016). Retrieved from http://www.okstate.com/news/2015/8/26/FB_0826152504.aspx?path=football

Board of Supervisors for Louisiana State University Agricultural and Mechanical College v. Smack Apparel Co., 550 F.3d 465 (2008).

Bornstein, R. F. (1989). Exposure and affect: Overview and meta-analysis of research 1968–1987. *Psychological Bulletin, 106*(2), 265–289.

Bosch, J., Venter, E., Han, Y. & Boshoff, C. (2006). The impact of brand identity on the perceived brand image of a merged higher education institution: Part Two. *Management Dynamics, 15*(3), 36–47.

Cacioppo, J. T. & Petty, R. E. (1979). Effects of message repetition and position on cognitive response, recall, and persuasion. *Journal of Personality and Social Psychology, 37*(1), 97–107. doi: 10.1037/0022-3514.37.1.97

Can I legally get myself tattooed with a pro sports team's logo? (2011, April 8). *The Straight Dope.* Retrieved from http://www.straightdope.com/columns/read/2990/can-i-legally-get-myself-tattooed-with-a-pro-sports-teams-logo

Carlson, C. (2016, September 9). Carrier Dome renovations will include air conditioning. Retrieved from http://www.syracuse.com/orangesports/index.ssf/2016/09/carrier_dome_renovations_will_include_air_conditioning.html

Carlson, C. (2016, May 2). Carrier Dome renovation: Can Syracuse University correct $1 million mistake? Retrieved from http://www.syracuse.com/orangesports/index.ssf/2016/05/carrier_dome_renovation_syracuse_university_may_be_able_to_correct_1_million_mis.html

Chase, C. (2015, November 20). Bill Belichick's real reason for dressing like a schlub on the sidelines. *USA Today.* Retrieved from http://ftw.usatoday.com/2015/11/bill-belichicks-sweatshirt-cutoff-buy-why-does-he-wear-it-reason-nike-origin

Cherry, K. (2009). Color Psychology: How Colors Impact Moods, Feelings, and Behaviors. Retrieved from http://psychology.about.com/od/sensationandperception/a/colorpsych.htm

Childers, T. L. & Houston, M. J. (1984). Conditions for a picture-superiority effect on consumer memory. *Journal of Consumer Research, 11*(2) 643–654.

Cianfrone, Tranova & Lee (In Press).

Clayton, M. J., Cavanagh, K. V. & Hettche, M. (2012). Institutional branding: a content analysis of public service announcements from American universities. *Journal of Marketing for Higher Education, 22*(2), 182–205. doi: 10.1080/08841241.2012.737869

CLC.com. (2017). *Licensing Information.* Retrieved from https://www.clc.com/Licensing-Info.aspx

Cole, B. (2016, February 10). Red Sox truck heading to Southwest Florida for spring training. *WINK News.* Retrieved from http://www.winknews.com/2016/02/10/red-sox-truck-heading-to-southwest-florida-for-spring-training/

Coleman, D. A. (2011). Service brand identity: definition, measurement, dimensionality and influence on brand performance. PhD Thesis, University of Birmingham.

Collange, V. (2015). Consumer reaction to service rebranding. *Journal of Retailing and Consumer Services, 22*, 178–186.

Craik, F. & Lockhart, R. (1972). Levels of processing: A framework for memory research. *Journal of Verbal Learning & Verbal Behavior, 11*, 671–684.

Curtis, C. (2017, February 27). Dumb Crystal Palace soccer fans accidentally vandalized their own team's bus. *USA Today.* Retrieved from http://ftw.usatoday.com/2017/02/crystal-palace-soccer-fans-vandalize-own-bus-middlesbrough-photos

Davis, R. (2013, July 15). USPTO Nixes Post-Bombing 'Boston Strong' Trademark Bids. Retrieved from http://www.law360.com/articles/457229/uspto-nixes-post-bombing-boston-strong-trademark-bid

Deakin University (2013). Brand Identity. Retrieved from http://www.deakin.edu.au/marketing/national-recruitment/comms-branding/brand-identity.php

Deflategate Timeline: After 544 days, Tom Brady Gives in. (2016, Jul 15). *ESPN.com.* Retrieved from http://www.espn.com/blog/new-england-patriots/post/_/id/4782561/timeline-of-events-for-deflategate-tom-brady

Dick, R. J. & Turner, B. A. (2007), Are fans and NBA marketing directors on the same page? A comparison of the value of marketing techniques. *Sport Marketing Quarterly, 16*, 140–146.

Dicker, R. (2013, April 22). 'Boston Strong' Trademark Race Begins; Two File Just Days After Boston Marathon Bombing. *Huffington Post.* Retrieved from http://www.huffingtonpost.com/2013/04/22/boston-strong-trademark_n_3131857.html. Accessed September 6, 2013.

Dondis, D. A. (1973). *A primer of brand literacy.* Cambridge, MA: MIT Press.

Dosh, K. (2012, Jan. 8). Cracking down on counterfeit apparel. *ESPN.com.* Retrieved from http://www.espn.com/blog/sec/post/_/id/36685/cracking-down-on-counterfeit-apparel-2

Dreyfus, H. (1972). *Symbol sourcebook: An authoritative guide to international graphic symbols.* New York: McGraw-Hill Book Company.

Duncan, T. & Moriarty, S. E. (2006). How integrated marketing communication's "touchpoints" can operationalize the service-dominant logic. In S. L. Vargo & R. F. Lusch (Eds.), *The Service Dominant Logic of Marketing: Dialog, Debate and Directions* (pp. 236–249). Armonk, New York: M.E. Sharpe.

Duncan, T. R. & Mulhern, F. (2004). A white paper on the status, scope and future of IMC. IMC Symposium co-sponsored by IMC programs at Northwestern University and University of Denver (March).

Eitzen, D.S. (2016). *Fair and foul: Beyond the myths and paradoxes of sport* (6th ed.). Lanham, MD: Rowman & Littlefield Publishing Group.

Eitzen, D. S. & Zinn, M. B. (2001). The dark side of sports symbols. *USA Today Magazine, 129*(2668), 48.

Erickson, R. A. (2012). Geography and the changing landscape of higher education. *Journal of Geography in Higher Education, 36*(1), 9–24. Doi: 10.1080/03098265.2012.651350

Farley, C. H. (2006, Summer). Why We Are Confused About Trademark Dilution Law. *Fordham Intellectual Property, Media & Entertainment Law Journal, 16*(4), 1175–1187.

Ferdous, A. S. (2008). Integrated Internal Marketing Communication (IIMC). The *Marketing Review, 8*(3), 223–235. doi: 10.1362/146934708X337654

Fetchko, M. J., Roy, D. P. & Clow, K. E. (2013). *Sports marketing.* Boston, MA: Pearson Education, Inc.

FindLaw for Legal Professionals. Retrieved from http://caselaw.findlaw.com/us-5th-circuit/1227156.html

Forsyth (In Press).

Forsyth & Lee (In Press).

Gartland, D. (2016, September 21). Saint Louis University has a new mascot and it's absolutely terrifying. Retrieved from http://www.si.com/extra-mustard/2016/09/21/saint-louis-billikens-new-mascot-photos

Gibbs, P. (2007). Does advertising pervert higher education? Is there a case for resistance? *Journal of Marketing for Higher Education, 17*(1), 3–11. doi: 10.1300/J050v17n01_02

Gladden, J. M. & Funk, D. C. (2001). Understanding brand loyalty in professional sport: examining the link between brand association and brand loyalty. *International Journal of Sports Marketing & Sponsorships, 3*(1), 67–94.

Gladden, J. M., Milne, G. R. & Sutton, W. (1998). A conceptual framework for assessing brand equity in Division I athletics. *Journal of Sports Management, 12*(1), 1–19.

Goldstone, D. J. & Toren, P .J. (1998). The criminalization of trademark counterfeiting. *Connecticut Law Review,* 31, 1–73.

Goolkasian, P. & Foos, P. W. (2002). Presentation format and its effect on working memory. *Memory & Cognition, 30,* 1096–1105.

Gregg, E. A., Pierce, D., Lee, J. W., Himstedt, L. & Felver, N. (2013). Giving UE a new (F)Ace. *Journal of Issues in Intercollegiate Athletics, 6,* 155–173. Retrieved from http://csrijiia.org/documents/puclications/research_articles/2013/JIIA_2013_6_9_155_173_A_New_Ace.pdf

Grossman, G. (1994). Carefully crafted identity can build brand equity. *Public Relations Journal, 50*(8), 18–21.

Harris, M. S. (2009). Message in a bottle: University advertising during bowl games. *Innovative Higher Education, 33*(5), 285–296. doi: 10.1007/s10755-008-9085-9

Healey, T. (2014, Feb. 8). Red Sox fans show support on annual Truck Day. MLB.com. Retrieved from http://m.mlb.com/news/article/67569480/red-sox-fans-brave-cold-on-annual-truck-day/

Henderson, P. W. & Cote, J. A. (1998). Guidelines for selecting or modifying logos. *Journal of Marketing, 62*(2), 14–30. http://www.jstor.org/stable/1252158

Henderson, P. W., Giese, J. L. & Cote, J. A. (2004). Impression management using typeface design. *Journal of Marketing, 68*(4), 60–72. doi: 10.1509/jmkg.68.4.60.42736

Hick, W. E. (1952). On the rate of gain of information. *Quarterly Journal of Experimental Psychology, 4*(1), 11–26.

Himmelsbach, A. (2010, Nov. 26). Colleges Tell High Schools Logos Are Off Limits. *New York Times.*

Historical Overview of the Academic Costume Code. (2017). American Council on Education. Retrieved from http://www.acenet.edu/news-room/Pages/Historical-Overview-Academic-Costume-Code.aspx

Hollingworth, H. L. (1913). Characteristic differences between recall and recognition. *The American Journal of Psychology, 24*(4), 532–544.

Holtzschue, L. (2006). *Understanding Color: An Introduction for Designers.* John Wiley & Sons.

Hull, Lee & Zapalac (In Progress).

Hussain, R. & Ferdous, A.S. (2014). Developing a framework of integrated brand brand identity touch-point (IVBIT) programmes in universities, *The Marketing Review, 14*(4), 431–445, doi: 10.1362/146934714X14185702841406

Hutchinson, M., Havard, C. T., Berg, B. K. & Ryan, T. D. (2016). Losing the core sport product: Marketing amidst uncertainty in college athletics. *Sport Marketing Quarterly, 25*(3), 185–194.

Hynes, N. (2009). Colour and meaning in corporate logos: an empirical study. *Journal of Brand Management, 16*(8), 545–555. doi: 10.1057/bm.2008.5

Itten, J. (1997). The Art of Color: The Subjective Experience and Objective Rationale of Color. John Wiley & Sons.

Jack LaLanne Biography. (2014). Retrieved from http://www.biography.com/people/jack-lalanne-273648#synopsis

Judson, K. M., Aurand, T. W., Gorchels, L. & Gordon, G. L. (2008). Building a university brand from within: university administrators' perspectives of internal branding. *Services Marketing Quarterly, 30*(1), 54–68. doi: 10.1080/15332960802467722

Kane, J. & Lee, J. W. (n.d.). "Physical fitness systems."

Kantanen, H. (2012). Identity, image and stakeholder dialogue. *Corporate Communications: An International Journal, 17*(1), 56–72. doi: 10.1108/13563281211196353

Keller, K. L. (1993). Measuring and conceptualising customer-based brand equity. *Journal of Marketing, 57*(1), 1–22. doi: 10.2307/1252054

Keller, K. L. (2007). *Building, measuring, and managing brand equity* (3rd ed). Upper Saddle River, NJ: Pearson.

Kessler, S. (2011). 7 ways universities are using facebook as a marketing tool. Retrieved from http://mashable.com/2011/10/17/facebook-marketing-collegesuniversities

Kitchen, P. J. & Schultz, D. E. (2003). Integrated corporate and product brand communication. *Advances in Competitiveness Research, 11*(1), 66–78.

Knight, J. (2013). The changing landscape of higher education internationalisation—for better or worse? *Perspectives: Policy and Practice in Higher Education, 17*(3), 84–90. doi: 10.1080/13603108.2012.753957

Korkidis, J. (2012, July 26). Infographic: Major League Baseball Teams And Their Pantone Colors. *Complex*. Available online at: http://www.complex.com/style/2012/07/infographic-major-league-baseball-teams-and-their-pantone-colors. Accessed January 24, 2018.

Lavrusik, V. (2009). 10 ways universities share information using social media. Retrieved from http://mashable.com/2009/07/15/social-media-public-affairs/

Lee, H. D. & Park, C. W. (2007). Conceptualization and measurement of multidimensionality of integrated marketing communications. *Journal of Advertising Research, 47*(3), 222–236.

Lee, J. W. (2011a). Logo. In L. E. Swayne & M. Dodds (Eds.), *Encyclopedia of Sports Management and Marketing* (Vol. 2, pp. 778–780). Thousand Oaks, CA: SAGE Reference.

Lee, J. W. (2011b). Mascots. In L. E. Swayne & M. Dodds (Eds.), *Encyclopedia of Sports Management and Marketing* (Vol. 2, pp. 867–869). Thousand Oaks, CA: SAGE Reference. Retrieved from http://link.galegroup.com.dax.lib.unf.edu/apps/doc/CX1959600446/GVRL?u=jack91990&sid=GVRL&xid=1e77955e

Lee, J. W. (2011c). New Orleans Saints. In L. E. Swayne & M. Dodds (Eds.), *Encyclopedia of Sports Management and Marketing* (Vol. 3, pp. 986–988). Thousand Oaks, CA: SAGE Reference.

Lee, J. W. (2011d). Tagline. In L. E. Swayne & M. Dodds (Eds.), *Encyclopedia of Sports Management and Marketing* (Vol. 4, pp. 1519–1520). Thousand Oaks, CA: SAGE Reference.

Lee, J. W. & Alessandri, S. W. (2014, February). "Boston Strong" but not trademark strong. Sport and Recreation Law Association (SRLA) Conference on Sport, Physical Activity, Recreation and Law, Orlando, FL.

Lee, J. W., Bernthal, M. J., Whisenant, W. & Mullane, S. (2010). NASCAR: Checkered flags are not all that are being waved, *Sport Marketing Quarterly, 19*(3), 110–117.

Lee, J. W. & Cavanaugh, T. (2016). Self-branding reflection through the use of infographic résumés. *Sport Management Education Journal, 10*(1), 78–85.

Lee, Cavanagh & Alessandri (In Press).

Lee, J. W., Conrad, K. & Thomas, D. (2013). Track and field and ethnic diversity. In C. Cortés (Ed.), *Multicultural America: A multimedia encyclopedia.* (pp. 2083–2085). Thousand Oaks, CA: SAGE Reference.

Lee, J. & Laucella, P. (2011). Sport Celebrities. In L. E. Swayne & M. Dodds (Eds.), *Encyclopedia of Sports Management and Marketing* (Vol. 4, pp. 1428–1431). Thousand Oaks, CA: SAGE Reference.

Lee, J. W. & Miloch, K. (2011a). Brand Personality. In L. E. Swayne & M. Dodds (Eds.), *Encyclopedia of Sports Management and Marketing* (Vol. 1, pp. 155–156). Thousand Oaks, CA: SAGE Reference.

Lee, J. W. & Miloch, K. (2011b). Player as Brand. In L. E. Swayne & M. Dodds (Eds.), *Encyclopedia of Sports Management and Marketing* (Vol. 3, pp. 1126–1128). Thousand Oaks, CA: SAGE Reference.

Lee, J. W., Miloch, K., Kraft, P. & Tatum, L. (2008). What's in a name? Building the brand through collegiate athletics at Troy University. *Sport Marketing Quarterly, 17*(3), 178–182.

Lee, J. & Sweeney, K. (2011). Jacksonville Jaguars. In L. E. Swayne & M. Dodds (Eds.), *Encyclopedia of Sports Management and Marketing* (Vol. 2, pp. 711–712). Thousand Oaks, CA: SAGE Reference.

Lee, J. W. & Whisenant, W. (2011). Anthems/Flag Raising. In L. E. Swayne & M. Dodds (Eds.), *Encyclopedia of Sports Management and Marketing* (Vol. 1, pp. 65–66). Thousand Oaks, CA: SAGE Reference.

Lee, J. W. & Whisenant, W. (2011). Petty Enterprises. In L. E. Swayne & M. Dodds (Eds.), *Encyclopedia of Sports Management and Marketing* (Vol. 3, pp. 1103–1104). Thousand Oaks, CA: SAGE Reference.

Lee, J. W., Wilson, M. & Gregg, E. A. (In Press). Learning from academic branding: Exploring institutional enhancement, visual identity, and the role of football. *Journal of School Public Relations, 37*(1), 113–144.

Lee, Zapalac & Godfrey (Under Review).

Lloyd, S. & Woodside, A.G. (2013). Corporate Brand-Rapture Theory: Antecedents, Processes, and Consequences. *Marketing Intelligence & Planning, 31*(5), 472–488. doi: 10.1108/MIP-04-2013-0064

Madhavaram, S., Badrinarayanan, V. & McDonald, R.E. (2005). Integrated marketing communication (IMC) and brand identity as critical components of brand equity strategy: A conceptual framework and research propositions. *Journal of Advertising, 34*(4), 69–80. doi: 10.1080/00913367.2005.10639213

Mahoney, K., Esckilsen, L. A., Jeralds, A. & Camp. S. (2015). *Public assembly venue management: Sports, entertainment, meeting, and convention venues.* International Association of Venue Managers: Coppell, TX.

Masiki, T. (2011). Academic brand Identity (AVI): An act of symbolic leadership. *Journal of Marketing for Higher Education, 21*(1), 85–105.

McNulty, J. A. (1965). An analysis of recall and recognition processes in verbal learning. *Journal of Verbal Learning and Verbal Behavior, 4*(5), 430–436.

Meir, R. & Scott, D. (2007). Tribalism: definition, identification and relevance to the marketing of professional sports franchises. *International Journal of Sports Marketing & Sponsorship, 8*(4), 330–346.

Meyer, K. A. (2008a). The virtual face of institutions: What do home pages reveal about higher education? *Innovative Higher Education, 33*(3), 141–157.

Mick and Susie McMurry High Altitude Performance Center Groundbreaking Held Saturday, 2016). Retrieved from http://www.gowyo.com/news/mick-and-susie-mcmurry-high-altitude-performance-center-groundbreaking-held-saturday-10-29-2016)

Miller, G. A. (1956). The magical number seven, plus or minus two: Some limits on our Mourad, M., Ennew, C. & Kortam, W. (2011). Brand equity in higher education. *Marketing Intelligence & Planning, 29*(4), 403–420. doi:10.1108/02634501111138563

The Most Outrageous Golf Clothes You Can Buy (2014, November 14). Retrieved from http://www.bloomberg.com/news/videos/2014-11-18/the-most-outrageous-golf-clothes-you-can-buy

Mullin, B. J., Hardy, S. & Sutton, W. (2000). *Sports Marketing.* Champaign, IL: Human Kinetics Press.

Nandan, S. (2005). An exploration of the brand identity—brand image linkage: a communications perspective. *The Journal of Brand Management, 12*(4), 264–278. doi: 10.1057/palgrave.bm.2540222

Nassar, M. A. (2012). An investigation of hoteliers' attitudes toward the use of social media as a branding tool. *International Journal of Marketing Studies, 4*(4), 93–105. doi: 10.5539/ijms.v4n4p93

New Billiken Mascot Makes Debut. (2016). Retrieved from http://www.slu.edu/news/2016/september/new-billiken-mascot-debuts.php

Newcomb, T. (2014). Ballpark Quirks: How Fenway Park's iconic Green Monster was born. *Sports Illustrated.* Available online at: https://www.si.com/mlb/strike-zone/2014/04/04/ballpark-quirks-fenway-park-green-monster-boston-red-sox. Accessed January 24, 2018.

Olympic Museum. The Olympic symbols. Retrieved from https://stillmed.olympic.org/Documents/Reports/EN/en_report_1303.pdf

Oregon State Media Guide—TBA.

Palmer, J. W. & Griffith, D. A. (1998). Information intensity: a paradigm for understanding web-site design. *Journal of Marketing Theory and Practice, 6*(3), 38–42.

Pavitt, M. (2016, May 10). IOC back Olympic Rings tattoos at Rio 2016 after swimmer's disqualification. Retrieved from http://www.insidethegames.biz/articles/1037316/ioc-back-olympic-rings-tattoos-at-rio-2016-after-swimmers-disqualification. Accessed February 28, 2017.

Pechmann, C. & Stewart, D. W. (1988). Advertising repetition: a critical review of wearin and wearout. *Journal of Current Issues and Research in Advertising, 11*(1–2), 285–330. doi: 10.1080/01633392.1988.10504936

Penn State Scandal Fast Facts. (2016, November 8). *CNN.* Retrieved from http://www.cnn.com/2013/10/28/us/penn-state-scandal-fast-facts/

Radford Athletics. (2016). Radford athletics unveils new logos. Retrieved from http://www.ruhighlanders.com/news/2016/10/13/ru-athletics-radford-athletics-unveils-new-logos.aspx?path=general (no longer available)

Read, J. D. & Barnsley, R. H. (1977). Remember Dick & Jane? Memory for elementary school readers. *Canadian Journal of Behavioral Science, 9*(4), 361–370.

Rein, I., Kotler, P. & Sheilds, B. (2006). *The Elusive fan: Reinventing sports in a crowded marketplace.* New York: McGraw-Hill.

Relive History. (2017). Retrieved from http://www.goodyearblimp.com/relive-history/#page/66.

Rogers, Y. (1989). Icons at the interface: Their usefulness. *Interacting with Computers, 1*(1) 105–117.

Rovell, D. (2017, February 12). Patriots look to next year, file for 'Blitz for Six' trademark. *ESPN.com.* Retrieved from http://www.espn.com/nfl/story/_/id/18670800/new-england-patriots-file-blitz-six-trademark

Rumpakis, A., Bee, C. & Lee, J. W. (Under Review). When it comes to rebranding, leave it to the Beavers: Transforming the brand identity of Oregon State University. *Journal of School Public Relations.*

Schechter, F. I. (1927). The rational basis of trademark protection. *Harvard Law Review*, 40, 813–833.

Schultz, D.E., S.I. Tannenbaum & R.F. Lauterborn. (1993). *Integrated marketing communications: Pulling it together and making it work.* Chicago: NTC Business Books.

Shabandri, M. (2012, September 24). Higher education: Will demand meet supply? Khaleej Times. Retrieved from http://www.khaleejtimes.com/DisplayArticle08.asp?xfile=data/education/2012/September/education_September4.xml§ion=education

Shostack, G. L. (1977). Breaking free from product marketing. *Journal of Marketing, 41*(2), 73–80. Retrieved from http://www.jstor.org/stable/1250637

Smith, R. A. & Schwartz, N. (2003). Language, social comparison, and college football: Is your school less similar to the rival school than the rival school is to you school? *Communication Monographs, 70*, 351–360.

Song, H. & Schwarz, N. (2008). If it's hard to read, it's hard to do: Processing fluency affects effort prediction and motivation. *Psychological Science, 19*(10), 986–988.

Sweeney, K. & Lee, J. W. (2014, February). The Super Bowl of criminal jocks: Investigating criminal incidents in the NFL. Sport and Recreation Law Association (SRLA) Conference, Orlando, FL.

Sweller, J. (1988). Cognitive load during problem solving: Effects on learning, *Cognitive Science, 12,* 257–285.

Tellis, G. J. (1997). Effective frequency: one exposure or three factors? *Journal of Advertising Research, 37*(4), 75–80.

Theriot, J. (2014). How the Tigers Got Their Colors. Available online at https://sites01.lsu.edu/wp/admissions/2014/02/25/5223/. Accessed February 2, 2018.

Trustees Univ. of Ark. v. Professional Therapy Serv., 873 F. Supp. 1280 (W.D. Ark. 1995).

UNC-Chapel Hill Web site. (2004, September 22). Trademark licensing revenue totals $3.7 million for fiscal 2004; UNC is nation's top performer. Retrieved from http://www.unc.edu/news/archives/sept04/liscense092204.html

Universities Australia (2013). A smarter Australia: an agenda for Australian higher education 2013–2016. Retrieved from http://www.voced.edu.au/content/ngv55503

University Colors. (2014). Retrieved from http://www.unc.edu/about/history-and-traditions/university-colors/

University of Wisconsin Office of Trademark Licensing Web site. Retrieved from licensing.wisc.edu/overview.html

Upshaw, L. B. (1995). *Building Brand Identity: A Strategy for Success in a Hostile Market Place.* New York: Wiley.

Use of Third Party Trademarked Names and Logos. (2017). Retrieved from http://www.littleleague.org/learn/rules/position statements/UsingTrademarkedNamesLogos.htm

van den Bosch, A. L., de Jong, M. D. & Elving, W. J. (2005). How corporate brand identity supports reputation. *Corporate Communications: An International Journal, 10*(2), 108–116. doi: 10.1108/13563280510596925

Wallace-McRee (In Press).

Wallström, Å., Karlsson, T. & Salehi-Sangari, E. (2008). Building a Corporate Brand: The Internal Brand Building Process in Swedish Service Firms. *Journal of Brand Management, 16*(1), 40–50. doi: 10.1057/bm.2008.18

Wakefield, K. (2016). *Team sports marketing* (2nd ed.). (eBook). Retrieved from www.teamsportsmarketing.com

Wei, W. (2010, July 21). Tiger Woods Lost $22 Million In Endorsements in 2010. Retrieved from http://www.businessinsider.com/tiger-woods-lost-22-million-in-2010-endorsements-2010-7

Wheeler, A. (2006). *Designing brand identity.* New York: John Wiley & Sons.

Williams, J. (2007). "Your Brand's True Colors" Retrieved from https://www.entrepreneur.com/article/175428

Wilson, L. (1998). *The trademark guide: A friendly guide to protecting and profiting from trademarks.* New York: Allworth Press.

Wu, F. & Lee, Y. K. (2005). Determinants of e-communication adoption: the internal push versus external pull factors. *Marketing Theory, 5*(1), 7–31. doi: 10.1177/1470593105049599

Zajonc, R. B. (1968). Attitudinal effects of mere exposure. *Journal of Personality and Social Psychology, 9*(2), 1–27.

Zimmer, B. (2013, May 12). "Boston Strong," the phrase that rallied a city. *Boston Globe*. Retrieved from http://www.bostonglobe.com/ideas/2013/05/11/boston-strong-phrase-that-rallied-city/uNPFaI8Mv4QxsWqpjXBOQO/story.html

Index

Pages with tables are indicated by "T" followed by the page number.